In the fish bowl

MINISTERS' CHILDREN
& THE LIVES THEY LEAD

STEVE MALTEMPI

ISBN-13: 978-1502770479
ISBN-10: 1502770474

Subject Heading: PASTOR'S/CHILDREN/FAMILY

Library of Congress Control Number: 2014918242
CreateSpace Independent Publishing Platform, North Charleston, SC

DEDICATION

To our four children who were raised as minister's children—Joe, Rebekah, Abigail and Jonathan. Each of them was and is an amazing child in their own right. Each was student of the year at their respective school. They were great examples and leaders among their peers at church, school and in the community. They were not perfect, but they were the kind of minister's children who made us proud. Each has experienced great blessings and difficulties in the church and as a minister's child. Each of them handled things differently. They have established and enjoyed great friendships. They know the church is not perfect, but still love attending church and serving others.

ABOUT THE AUTHOR

"In the Fishbowl" is the culmination of more than 24 years of being a minister with children of his own and personally working with many ministers and their children. Steve and Joy Maltempi have been married for more than 31 years. They have four children that have all grown up in the church and carried the title "Minister's Child." Steve has been a pastor for students in churches in Louisiana, Virginia, and Texas. He has served as the statewide student and collegiate ministry strategist and associate in Virginia. He currently works as the Collegiate and Student Ministry Lead Associate for the Southern Baptists of Texas Convention. He is gifted in his work as he consults and counsels with student and collegiate pastors. He continues to lead student ministry and affect the lives of thousands of students. Steve has written an intelligent and challenging book with humor and straightforward language.

Steve graduated from Louisiana Tech University with a bachelor's degree in business management, from New Orleans Baptist Theological Seminary with a master's degree in Christian education and from Oxford

Graduate School with a doctor of philosophy. Joy Maltempi graduated from Louisiana Tech University with a bachelor's degree in business data systems management. Steve's children are normal and well-adjusted. Their children were schooled at home, in private Christian schools, and in public schools. During high school they cheered, played sports, and were normal adolescents. Each child was selected as a student of the year during his or her time in public school.

Steve's oldest child, Joe, played football for LSU, has received his bachelor's degree in chemical engineering and has a great job and wife. Their oldest daughter, Rebekah, graduated from LSU with a major in kinesiology and a minor in Spanish. She is very involved in missions and is married. Their third child, Abigail, graduated from high school with a state license in cosmetology. Abigail spent four months in Budapest, Hungary during the fall of 2013. She wants to pursue a degree in biblical studies, go to seminary and return to the mission field. Their fourth child, Jonathan, was a sophomore in high school when he lost his six and a half year battle with brain tumors. Jonathan passed away February 1, 2013. He was very funny and bright, and the sky was NOT the limit for him—he is in Heaven!
Steve and Joy have done an inspiring job of raising their children to have faith in the Lord. The church has seen each Maltempi child grow into a faith of their own, able to stand on their own faith experiences and loving life and the people around them. Their children continue to be a joy to their parents and to all those that know them.

The Maltempi's children love their family and have felt privileged to have a loving church family as well. As they grew up, the children looked forward to church and enjoyed seeing God do his work. This is their wish for all!

Steve has written, "Our family has experienced most of what is written here, but this book is not about our children. It is about every child of a minister."

TABLE OF CONTENTS

PREFACE

There are stories throughout this book, told from the perspective of the children of ministers, some of who are now adults. These stories are humorous as well as horrendous; delightful and detestable; and, some are downright mean-spirited.

Perhaps in the future, ministers' children will be viewed as who they truly are: individual people, created in God's image, who are spiritually mature followers of Christ. Their success will be understood as an accomplishment and acknowledged as a personal achievement.

If you are an MC (ministers child), you will be encouraged to know you are not alone in your journey. After reading these pages, you will likely think to yourself, "It sounds like we were all members of the same church!" For now, relax and read what it is like to be the child of a minister, for in these pages you will think someone has been reading your mind, recording your thoughts and actions. You will come to understand that the stereotypes people have concerning the children of ministers are mostly false. Most

MCs are great people that are well adjusted and socially adept. As an MC, you should be proud of who you are in relation to your father and who you are becoming as an individual.

I have served in four churches alongside many staff members with children and watched those children react differently to their dad's ministry. I have also watched ministers' wives deal with their husband's victories and failures. There were times of great joy and times of deep sorrow. Each of the minister's family members was supported and attacked differently. That does not happen in the corporate world. If people don't like the CEO's child, they don't dare say anything to the child or to the CEO. In a church, people seem to think it is their right to press their own ideas on the minister's child(ren). Each minister, minister's wife and child reacted within their personality—sometimes appropriately and sometimes inappropriately. The children reacted just as they should—as a maturing person. Sometimes the teenage MC reacted with wisdom, and sometimes their immaturity was on display. Usually, the wives were graceful under fire, but not always. The families of ministers are only human, and they, just like church members, from time to time, misbehave. Sounds normal doesn't it? It is normal, except in the eyes of many church members who expect perfect behavior, personality, spirituality, leadership, example, biblical knowledge and a whole host of perfect human qualities from ministers, ministers' wives, and MCs.

My family was and is no different from any other. In the end, we all want our children to have fond memories of their childhood as a minister's child. We all have glory days we remember fondly. Such as when we drive past our old high school football stadium where we had winning seasons. Or when we drive past our favorite fishing spot. When we drive past our favorite college or pro team's stadium where we watched our team win. We remember those things and point them out to our children. When the MC drives past the church where his or her dad ministered, what will they remember? These churches become their homes—their home away from home—where they sit and wait while their dad finishes endless business meetings, prayer meetings, cleaning the church, talking to people, counseling people, etc. It is my prayer for all ministers' children to have fond memories to tell their children. I pray they will remember the victories and grace of Christ that is on us all and not merely all they endured as a minister's child.

INTRODUCTION

What is it like to be a minister's child (MC)? If you are a minister, throughout the pages of this book you will find stories and ideas familiar to you and your family. If you are not a minister, this book will be fascinating and help you discover and understand the life of a minister's child. This will be a fresh perspective on people with whom you have been friends and whom you have seen grow up—ministers' children, young and old. These people are real, with real feelings, real needs, real goals and real aspirations. MCs would love you to have a deeper understanding of who they are and the issues they navigate.

When beginning to write this book, I struggled with what to call the minister's child. Should they be called the preacher's child or PK? This book deals with more than just the preacher's child. It deals with the children of all ministers, student ministers, music ministers, education ministers, children's ministers, missionaries and so forth. The parents of missionary children have been called by God as well, except to a foreign country. Missionaries' children deal with much of the same situations as local church ministers' children do, except they are isolated from a familiar culture and family. Plus, many times they are in danger.

MCs are people too! Their fathers, men of God, do all kinds of ministry on a full-time and part-time basis in the church. Their dads are ordained by a church and licensed by a state. Being ordained by a church means the church recognizes the prospective minister is called out and being separated for ministry by God. These ministers will dedicate their professional lives to minister within and for a church body.

I challenge you to get to know MCs for who they are rather than through the lens of their father's image. I believe you will be pleasantly surprised to find a thriving heart longing to be recognized as an individual with talents and gifts.

This book focuses specifically on the fishbowl effect as it relates to the children of ministers. It does not focus on how ministers' children behave. However, after reading this book you will have a new appreciation for ministers, their wives and their children. Ministers have goals for their children—that they grow up normal, well-adjusted, healthy and loving God and others as they glorify God. Can we ask more?

CHAPTER ONE
BEING AN MC IS A BIG DEAL!

What is the fish bowl concept?

The children of ministers and other children whose parents are popular, on-stage regularly, famous, infamous, or otherwise well known by large numbers of the public, live a different kind of life—especially those children who mingle among their parent's followers or fans. These children have the eyes of many watching their every move –how they dress, behave, misbehave, with whom they associate, daily schedules, favorite colors and foods, hair styles and how they talk, to name a few. People they have never met or about whom they know very little seem to know intimate details of their lives. They are in plain sight of many people. Not only are they in plain sight, but they are in ear shot of hearing not only their own positive traits and faults but that of their parent(s), as well, especially their father, the minister. They live in a fishbowl surrounded by glass. **They have no place to hide—nothing to hide behind or to camouflage their being. Their lives are unwittingly on display for all to see.** People observing MCs develop ideas according to their own presuppositions on politics, religion, morals, lifestyles, economics and a host of other life situations. Many times the judgments of church members are skewed through their own family and cultural lens.

What is one to do when they are born into a situation they have to live up to? When do MCs get to be who they were created to be, to follow their passions, their sense of individuality and the expectations they set for themselves? What happens when MCs don't live up to the expectations of not only their parents, but of church members and society? **Do MCs— should MCs—base their self-worth and success in their formative years on the feedback of church members?** MCs are born into the fish bowl with everyone having access to their lives. It is like seeing Jim Carey in *The Truman Project*. It is a true life reality show lived out by millions of ministers' children and families every day. The children of ministers don't wake up one day and decide to put their lives on display for the world to see and judge, yet that is the reality with which they live.

MCs fathers' jobs give them a certain amount of notoriety which can be as much to their detriment as to their well-being. The size of the church and town matters little. Minister's children in small churches in small towns are identified quickly. The small town's eyes are upon them. There is a great similarity to any celebrity or well-known person moving to a small town with their children. Word quickly spreads about the children—who they are, what they look like and facts and perceptions about them. On the other extreme, a pastor with children may become the pastor of a large church with influence in the community. Once again, word spreads quickly about the children. Children with parents in other professions can come and go with little notice. This is usually not the case with the minister's child.

Children are all noticed for different reasons. It may be because they are a good student, have a magnetic personality or are a good athlete. Ministers' children are deemed extraordinary not because of themselves, but because of their father. This can be a hard reality to deal with, when realized. For a minister's child to find out that everyone is nice to them or likes them, not because of who they are, but because of whom their parent is, can be crushing. MCs are popular often because of their parent, not because of their own talents, personality, skills, gifts strengths and weaknesses. Likewise, for a minister's child to find everyone is not nice to them, not because of whom they are, but because of who their parent is, can be crushing. Can you imagine finally figuring out in 7th or 8th grade that other's behavior toward you has all been because of who your parent is and not because of who you are? It is no wonder that many MCs get close to only a few friends they can trust, who love them for who they are and not because their dad is a minister. The same can be said of popular athletes, celebrities, politicians and millionaires. People attach to them to get close to their parents, because of who their parent is and because of perceived perks of being associated with the child of a well-known person. MCs must learn how to choose their friends. They must learn that it is not mean or arrogant to be picky about whom they let connect to them as a friend. Yes, MCs should always be nice, but they need to choose friends who love them because of who they are and not because of their father's position. Most MCs find great friends in other

MCs, just as many celebrity's children find friends whose parents are in a similar situation.

It is hoped this book will be the voice of the millions of ministers' children. Only the child of a minister knows what it is like. This book is written for the children of ministers, ministers, congregants and others. The children of ministers need to know their problems and blessings are common and they are not alone. Ministers need to understand their children better. Congregants need to take steps to treat ministers children like every other child and teenager.

The idea that became this book began with seeing how my own children had dealt with being a child of a minister. I saw each of them deal with it in their own way. As I began searching for material on this subject, I found very little. The book I did find detailed the special situations of the children of nationally and world renowned celebrities such as sports stars, movie stars, TV stars and politicians. It was striking how many issues they dealt with that ministers' children deal with as well. Ministers' children are not on the edge of the spotlight like a celebrity, but they are just off the platform, in his shadows! The children of ministers are just as vulnerable as other famous people because they are in the presence of their dads' "public" several times each week. Not only are they in church around church members, but they cannot miss a service unless they are away on vacation. There is no escape from their father's public. Movie stars and other famous parents can shield their children and hide them away in gated communities, private homes and vacation properties around the world. Ministers have no such luxury.

MCs see and hear all the good and bad about their dad personally from people that are close to them, from church members and from people in the community. The difference between superstars and pastors is that pastors minister in national obscurity and most of the time below or at the poverty level. Ministers who are at a church with a decent salary have to be careful about how much they communicate about what they do and where they go on vacation. What is perceived by the minister as a normal vacation amenity will certainly be seen by some church members as extravagant. After all, ministers minister to all socio-economic levels. And each level is biblically committed to tithe (give a 10th of their income) to the church. Part of that goes towards the pastor's salary. Hard working folks don't like it when the pastor gets to enjoy vacations that are much nicer than the average church member. So, ministers and their children don't need to share all of the details of their vacations, when they eat out or what the family does away from the church. Ministers sacrifice a lot to minister to their congregation. This is a good time to remember that pastors are called by God—24 hours a day, 7 days a week. There is no switch to turn on their calling at 8am when they go to work and turn it off at 5pm when they go home. These office hours for a pastor are myth anyway. So, when the pastor and his family get a chance to get away, they need to completely separate themselves from congregational expectations and demands. This doesn't mean they turn off their Christian lifestyle.

MCs are encouraged by church member's positive comments and acts of love towards their dad. However, they are also discouraged when church members do the opposite—especially when the negative comments are unfounded, negatively skewed, misunderstood or a downright lie. Ministers' children don't have paparazzi chasing them, but they do have church members watching their every move and word for mistakes. Ministers' children do not have to worry about their stories being published in tabloids. But their stories are spun into half-truths as they go through the church gossip mill. Church members are free to critique the ministers' children on a variety of subjects ranging from how they dress, wear make-up, act in church, behave in public, know the Bible, understand politics and how they choose friends, just to name a few. Pastors and their wives must set boundaries for the congregation. Boundaries must be set and reinforced often among church leaders and from the pulpit. There must be balance between nagging the MCs and encouraging them to live a lives worthy of being called Christian. In general, church members should never comment directly to the MC about how they are dressed, where they sit in church, how they play a sport (aggressive or not), if they date or who they date, among other things. These should be left to the parent. On the other hand, bad behavior, like disrespecting an elder and not doing what they are told by a congregant should be dealt with just as it would with any other child.

So the questions are: What is it like to be the child of a minister? How do we as ministers help our children deal with our profession and calling? What can we do to help them mature into well-adjusted Christian adults that love the Lord and His bride, the church? How does being the child of a pastor affect their children? What do MCs like and dislike about being a pastor's child? What do MCs feel their parents did right/wrong? How can we help MCs and ministers in their journey? What are some of the positive and negative experiences of MCs?

QUESTIONS TO CONSIDER

For the Church Member:

1. List the MCs you have known.

2. Beside each name – list their positive and negative behaviors and influences.

3. Have you mirrored your love for or disdain towards a minister's child because of their father?

4. As you read this book, write the name of the MC you relate to a particular idea.

5. Pray for the MCs with whom you have been associated.

For the Minister and his Wife

1. Which ideas in this chapter relate to your children the most?

2. What action steps will you take to help your children?

3. How will you educate your congregation?

CHAPTER TWO
MCs ARE NOT ALONE

What is it like to be a minister's child? Most children of ministers do not get asked this question directly. However, there are significant differences between the children of non-ministers and ministers. This book shows many situations in which MCs find themselves, both positive and negative. There are many advantages and disadvantages of being a minister's child. Most MCs can't describe what it is like to be a minister's child because they have never been anything else and have no basis for comparison. What they do know is that different expectations are placed upon them by church members. The MCs can feel like a fish in a bowl. Their lives are on display for the world to see and judge.

Of the many differences, advantages and disadvantages of being a minister's child, most deal with the same situations and questions. After leading a seminar specifically for MCs and hearing many MCs share stories about their personal experiences, one MC said, "It sounds like we all went to the same church." Church members are curious about how distinctive and special the life of a MC must be. What is it like to be a minister's child?

Do they really pray at every meal? Do they have family devotions every morning and night? Do they pray every time they get in the car to go somewhere? Do they read the Bible as a family every night? Do they only watch G-rated movies, or do they watch TV at all? Do they listen to non-Christian music? Do they talk in King James English around their house? The list is unending about what people silently and sometimes, not so silently, wonder about the life of a MC. The answers of the questions above are as different as the individuals answering them. Here is the general consensus to the above questions. Do they really pray at every meal? My experience tells me they pray at every meal whether at home or in public. Praying for a meal is not something they do to meet the expectations of congregants, but rather because they are truly thankful. Do they have family devotions every morning and night? Again, my experience is that they are fairly consistent with family devotions. Do they pray every time they get in the car to go somewhere? Not always. After all, bad driving is not cured by prayer. Do they only watch G-rated movies, or do they watch TV at all? They usually do not watch any movie with cussing, or otherwise mature content. Ministers know how to research the content of movies to avoid the language and sexual situations. They also are diligent to get software that filters content. Do they listen to non-Christian music? This is probably the most diverse behavior. I love listening to classic rock. However, while my children were young we made sure they were exposed to the best Christian concerts, then bought the music for them to listen to at home and in the car. They really never missed secular radio. Do they talk in King James English around their house? NO!

As Kathy Cronkite, daughter of Walter Cronkite, so wonderfully said, "The reality is there are times when it is extremely difficult and there are times when being the child of a celebrity (minister's child) is absolutely wonderful."[1]

Ministers, like other celebrities, are not perfect people. Because of their position as a pastor their reputation must be above reproach. Pastors' children are expected to be above reproach and well behaved. Behavior is important, but more important is the heart of the MC, for it is the heart that is desperately wicked. Ministers must demonstrate and teach a right heart as well as show right actions. Growing up as a child of a "celebrity," MCs experience both privileges and problems. The problem is that minister's children don't have a life of privilege and wealth to offset the problems. Not that wealth is the fix-all to problems, but it doesn't hurt either. MCs experiences are similar, to some degree, to those of children of all public figures, whether they are the children of politicians, sports stars, media stars, etc. MCs cope with their situations differently. To cope, some turn to self-destructive, at-risk behaviors such as drugs, alcohol, cutting or sex. Some do everything in their power to separate themselves from their father, his profession and his identity. It does not take much to tarnish one's reputation, so the pressure of being "perfect" is removed or limited. It is an interesting phenomenon, and heart-breaking, to watch an adolescent trade a good reputation for a tarnished reputation. Pastors need to recognize the beginning of a child destroying their good reputation. Once recognized, the pastor needs to remove their child from the pressure (or remove the pressure). Sometimes it only takes an outing and a little fun to get the

MC to open up and talk. When the MC opens up, the pastor must not make excuses or defend why it happened. The pastor must act on behalf of their child. After all, it is the MC with whom the pastor wants to have a life-long relationship, even more so than with the congregant. Most MCs want people to recognize them as a good person; however, once the bad reputation is established, it can take years to rebuild trust and credibility. The bad behavior may not ever be forgotten, but it will be forgiven.

The identity of being a minister's child is a weighty matter. Some MCs have been known to use an alias to avoid that awful question, "Are you any relation to…?" Some adult children of ministers put a lot of distance between themselves and their family and spend several years pursuing their own career. Along the way, they begin to figure out how their father's job has impacted them. Their father's job has impacted them as they have learned how to deal with people, have friends, manage finances, work hard, work smart, understand the importance of being their own person, stand for what is right and have an opinion that is contrary to public opinion. Many MCs come to terms with themselves and come to terms with themselves and who they are in relation to their father. It is important for MCs to sort out what it means to be a minister's child. When they go out into the world to make their own life, they begin to learn what effect their father's ministry, job, popularity (or not) has had on them, and they seek to identify ways to deal with it.

What do some staff children learn that others don't? How much Bible is enough? What do some parents say or do? How much church attendance is enough? What steps do some children take? What strengths do some have? Why do some not make it? Why do some turn completely away from the Lord? What can be done, said, explained or shared that would help the children of ministers not only survive, but thrive in their faith and family relationships? Let's stop and try to answer a few of these questions. What do some staff children learn that others don't? Every believer must develop a faith of their own. It does not matter if the individual is an MC or a regular church attending adolescent; they must have learned to trust in Christ in every situation. Sadly, most children, MCs or not, are coddled by parents and protected so much that they never have to depend on God for an answer or to get them through tough situations. I am not suggesting we leave our young to fend for themselves, but at the same time, we can't be their savior. Christ is their savior. This reminds me of a folk story about how American Indians raise their children. When an Indian infant crawled toward the fire in the teepee, the parent would not stop them from reaching out and touching or grabbing a hot coal. At first this sounds like bad parenting. However, the result is that the parent never had to tell the child not to touch the fire again and the minor burn healed. Again, balance and wisdom in parenting can help us to know when not to protect our children from a valuable lesson.

How much Bible is enough? Learning scripture is always profitable, for it never returns void. Scripture is like gold nuggets in a well of knowledge and wisdom from which the child can draw for the rest of his or her life. MCs and other Christian children should have read through the Bible several times before they graduate from high school. Not only should they have read through it several times, but they need to read it in several translations, chronologically, doctrinally, etc.

What do some parents say or do? Parents must say and do the right things consistently and their behavior must match what they say. Children need to see consistency from their parents as they teach what is expected of them as an MC and model appropriate behavior before them.

How much church attendance is enough? Can I say that sometimes too much is simply, too much, especially if the minister's home is like church? Not that the minister turns off Christianity when at home, but every conversation does not need to be a sermon or answered with scripture either. MCs need their dad to be their parent more than their minister. MCs will have many ministers in their lifetime, but they will only have two parents. My own children send emails to my church email address when they want a fast answer. They know I check my church email address all day long. However, when I reply, they ask me to replace the automatic email signature with "dad." I actually love taking a few extra seconds to change it to "dad."

What steps do some MCs take that others do not? What strengths do some have? All children handle things differently and have different strengths and weaknesses. It is the parent's responsibility to know each child and to help them navigate their reactions to situations and how they think about them.

Why do some turn completely away from the Lord? What can be done, said, explained or shared that would help the children of ministers not only survive, but thrive in their faith and family relationships? One can read through the Bible and be very frustrated how the children of prophets and other men of God turned their back on how they were raised. They can also be frustrated how the children of prophets turn their back on God. However, we can also see those that developed a faith of their own, like King David, who had a heart after that of God, did very well. Again, each person must develop their own faith. In today's society Christian young people continue to demonstrate the faith of an adolescent well into their twenties. Christianity needs to deviate sharply from the world's standards of maturity and do what is necessary to challenge our children to thrive in their faith.

QUESTIONS TO CONSIDER

For the Church Member

1. What are your preconceptions of ministers?

2. What are your preconceptions of MCs?

3. How should they differ?

4. Why should they differ?

5. How is being a minister the same and different from being a corporate leader?

6. How do you treat your boss differently than your pastor?

7. Why do you think MCs act in non-Christian ways?

For the Minister and his Wife

1. Do you share with your church family what you expect of your children and wife?

2. Do you share your expectations and set boundaries for the church about your family?

3. In what situations do your children think being a MC is amazing?

4. In what situations do your children think being a MC is the worst thing?

Bibliography

1. Cronkite, Kathy, On the Edge of the Spotlight, William Morrow & Co; 1981.

CHAPTER THREE
GROWING UP AS A MINISTER'S CHILD

"My dad is my dad first and my minister second," said one child of a minister. My first church was a small mission church in south Louisiana. There were about 150 members and there were four staff members—the pastor, myself as Student Pastor and a part-time secretary and custodian. I was attending New Orleans Baptist Theological Seminary and working odd jobs while praying for God to show us His will. Finally, this small church in Thibodaux, La. offered me a job as a student minister. My wife and I and were very excited about this opportunity. We immediately knew God was with us when meeting with the pastor and a family for dinner one night to pray about us joining the staff. After the meal, we all went into the living room and talked about ministry and got to know one another. Then the pastor asked us all to have a little prayer meeting in the living room, asking God to give us a clear understanding of His will for our lives regarding joining the staff. So there we were–my wife and I, our son (hyperactive, alert and very mobile) and our quiet, sleeping daughter. My wife and I were sitting on the couch with my son standing between my legs and daughter in a child carrier. My daughter had fallen asleep and was quiet during the prayer. To my amazement, over the next hour my son stood perfectly still and quiet with his head bowed and his eyes closed. Needless to say, the adults were impressed. So were my wife and I! My son had displayed, unknowingly, perfect MC behavior that helped me get the position as student minister. They thought, "Wow, what a well-behaved little boy. He must have been taught to be quiet and still during prayers." To this day, we laugh and are amazed our son stood still and quiet for an hour. Strange, isn't it, how expectations of ministers can be unrealistic. I would not have thought bad about my son if he had not stood still and quiet during the prayer. But, that was the expectation.

My first Sunday, I was sitting in the back of the sanctuary holding my son to keep him quiet. After all, minister's children must behave at all times, right? You may ask, "Where was your wife?" In the nursery of course, working! This is a common job for all minister's wives in small churches. It is not only expected, but demanded. The pastor called me to the front to make announcements, so I proceeded to put my son down on the pew so I could get up and go to the stage at the front of the sanctuary to make announcements. My son immediately clamped down on my arm and gave a cry of uncertainty and fear. So there I stood with my son in my arms not knowing what to do. As I looked at the pastor with questioning eyes, my pastor finally, after what seemed like an eternity and before I tried to peel my son off my arm, said, "Bring him with you and hold him while you make announcements." What a relief! So there we were, my son and I, on the platform making announcements. Once again, as if on cue, my son behaved perfectly to everyone's delight. Again…a huge relief! After all, word had gotten out about how well he behaved during the living room prayer time and he already had a good reputation to live up to. As much of a reputation as a 2 year old can have! On another occasion, this same child was picked up by the pastor and put on the pastor's hip while they talked. They had become friends and very acquainted. This particular pastor always had every hair in place and was proud of his looks. Without warning, my son reached up with both hands and messed up the pastor's hair before the pastor could stop him. Everyone, including the pastor, roared with laughter. This could have been a tense situation, but the pastor handled it perfectly. We didn't overreact, nor did the pastor. Our son's action was innocent and playful, expressed as such and received as such. It was my expectation that our children would have a special, up close relationship with other staff members and their families.

In that small church, every church member was like a favorite aunt, uncle or grandparent in the eyes of our children. Life can't get much better than that! Everyone knew their names, favorite color, pet, candy, allergy and seemingly every detail of their lives. MCs are doted upon much more so than other children attending the church. Each Sunday it seemed every person in the church loved on them by greeting them by name and smiling. Some church members greeted them with a piece of candy or mint every Sunday morning. It was as if they were greeting the child of a celebrity. Even people we had never met would call them by name, squat to their level, shake their hand, give them a high five or fondly scrub their little head. Many would walk out of their way to say, "hi," and give them a gift certificate for a free ice cream cone or root beer float. Life was good! As a minister, I didn't expect our children to be given special treatment; it just happened. As a minister, I had no right to expect special treatment. Ministers are also expected to let church members bless them and their children. When a minister does not accept a gift it is seen as rejecting not only the gift, but the person as well. It is seen as rejecting a blessing. It is hard to graciously decline a gift from a church member, and it is a no-win situation. This can also be the case when MCs receive unexpected gifts from church members. Other than special days, like birthdays, MCs don't understand the concept of not receiving gifts—gifts like a season pass to the theme park or tickets to a game or theater. When received, it must be done graciously, but not advertised as if one is bragging on the special gifts they receive. With hundreds or sometimes thousands of members, it can be a problem if not kept in check.

For us, as parents, we were simply trying to raise our children as we had been raised. My wife and I came from families with traditional beliefs. My parents were very involved in church leadership and where faithful church members. This background allowed me to know what church members expected of the children of their ministers. I had the privilege of knowing many very Christ-like MCs. They had maturity beyond their years and were perfect examples for the rest of us. I also knew a few MCs that had very "unchristian" lifestyles and behaviors. Some MCs nearly wrecked their dads' ministries, vocations and professions by their bad behavior. This bad behavior is a stereotype and not reality for most MCs. I didn't want my child to be one of those "bad" MCs. I knew they would not be perfect, and it is pretty normal for students to figure out for themselves what they believe and how they will live their lives. But at the same time, my goal was to raise children that really were able to set the example and be Christian leaders not only in the youth group, but in the community through being involved in school activities and the public in general. In reality, this goal falls short of our purpose while on earth. Our purpose is to bring glory to God. We didn't want to stop with just raising moral, well-adjusted successful children. At least, I would give them the skills and knowledge to glorify God, be successful, be well-adjusted and have meaningful relationships, if they so choose.

From the perspective of the MC, some stereotypes are very disconcerting. Can you imagine hearing descriptions (good and bad) of what your life should be like? As one church member said, "Oh, you are the minister's kid. You are probably the worst kid in the entire youth group." What a horrible comment. The truth is that every behavior, whether good, bad or really bad, of the MC is seen and broadcast around the church. Other children in the church, even deacons' children, can do and say whatever they want, and nobody dares to correct them. And, the church member's child does not become the talk of the church or school. Can you imagine growing up in an open toxic environment like this? Yet, this is the opinion of many people, even strangers. It is hard to believe that mature Christian church members will accept gossip as true, and as an MC, there is no way to fight it, no way to say, "That is not my family or me. Surely they are talking about someone else. Where did they get their facts? That is not who we are as MCs." This is where the MCs parents must step in, stop the gossip and correct the church members responsible for spreading the rumor and gossiping. Ministers cannot take the easy road and let the problem go away with time. Ministers must step in and have a strong voice to stop the perpetrator. Personally, I would rather lose a church member than allow them to continually attack my child.

Two stories illustrate how the children of ministers can be misunderstood. While at that first small church, we did many group building experiences. On one occasion I took the youth group camping and fishing. After we spent the afternoon catching fish, we fried them and had a feast! Then we had a worship service by the fire and had a little free time. During free time, the students had a blast playing capture the flag and talking around the fire. Sometime after midnight everyone settled in for the evening—girls on one side of the camp and boys on the other side. Some were in tents and some were not. Once again, life was good—the students were behaving. And to make matters even better, my pastor's three children, all girls, were on the trip. Their influence was great! There were also two other chaperons helping. I slept like a baby. The next morning, I woke up early and began noticing several students wandering toward the early morning fire and the smell of cooked bacon. I also noticed several students, both male and female coming from the barn. Apparently several had slept there most of the night. What I saw next terrified me. The pastor's daughters were coming out of the barn. Believe me when I say, both girls were as innocent as could be. But the appearance of them sleeping in a barn with others—both male and female, was not good. But knowing this group, I had no concerns of impropriety. They just thought it would be fun to sleep in the hay loft instead of sleeping on the hard ground. Actually, it was a good idea. But…it sure didn't look good. I knew immediately that the next day at church, members would say the pastor's daughters spent the night in the hayloft with boys. It was unfair and not the whole story. I did my best to defuse the situation. But, then, church members discounted what I said because they thought I was just trying to cover my own tail. I learned quickly that situations would happen and that there is no way to coach your children ahead of time to handle every situation the right way. It is the same in ministry. There are conflicts to deal with whether the youth group is growing or not, so you might as well have a youth group that is growing. You may as well get good at handling the problems associated with a growing group. When things like this happen it is wise to communicate with the MCs involved, their parents and church leaders. Only tell those that need to know. There is no need to tell the world what happened and try to explain the situation.

When my son was in ninth grade, he was a leader in the youth group and well liked. Just before the new school year, a new girl moved to town and began attending our youth group and church. For some reason, every time she would pass my son, she would hit him in the arm or stomach. He would say, "Stop, don't do that again," and move on. I always encouraged him not to hit a girl but to continue to tell her to stop. He demonstrated a lot of patience for months. After this continued for several months, I too, had enough. I told him the next time she hit him, to tell her that the next time she did it, he was going to hit her back with the same force. Sure enough, after church one Sunday we were at a friend's house with several students from the group. We were all in the living room together. As expected, she hit him, and right on cue, he hit her back (with the same force, which was considerable). Of course, she was very surprised and hurt and began crying. I think she was a little embarrassed as well. Immediately, another adult grabbed my son, took him to another room and began talking to him very firmly and a little angrily about his behavior and lack of restraint. He explained the situation but was still in trouble with the adult. I didn't get onto my son. Neither did I confront the adult that fussed at him. I appreciated her talking to him. I will not try to guess why the girl was hitting my son, but I am sure of one thing: she stopped hitting him. Yes, it was said by a few that my son was a bully. Even after months of asking her to stop, church members thought less of him because of his actions. It is interesting though, that many students in the youth group said they were glad he finally took up for himself and stopped taking the abuse.

In hindsight, I should not have told him to hit her. I should have stepped in and talked to the girl and her parents and stopped the behavior before it escalated to retaliation.

These are just two examples of situations with which MCs must deal. More will follow as different subjects are discussed.

The typical Sunday morning of a minister's family.

MCs rarely see their dad on Sunday morning, ride to church with him or sit with him during church. The pastor's wife always dresses herself and the children. She then loads them into the family car and drives them to church. When arriving at church every Sunday, it is like a grand presentation to the church members. She then distributes the children to their appropriate age group class. Then, she walks into her own Sunday School class as if her world is perfect and she is ready to minister to others. Remember, once at church, the pastor's wife and children must make time for each person that wants to greet them, remember their name(s), make eye contact with everyone, return or initiate a greeting and return the customary praise of others' children, all the while never being late. I remember one MC that was in 5th grade that didn't want to be late to Sunday School again. She got out of the car, ran across the parking lot, through the building, not saying, 'hi,' to everyone or waiting for them to get out of her way. Later a church member said that child was the worst ever. Apparently they were the "worst ever" because they ran past them without saying, 'hi.' Neither did they walk respectfully through the church; they ran. Thankfully, the pastor's wife had thick skin and didn't let the church member's expectations cause her to get onto her child. Of course, while dad is preaching, it is the mom that has to make sure her children are sitting in church like perfect angels and examples for the other children. Expectations are the root of disappointment and bitterness. When others don't meet our expectations, we are disappointed in them. Kept unchecked, the disappointment will lead to bitterness. This cycle must be broken through communication so expectations can be replaced by reality.

Every day of his or her life, an MC must dress, not according to their own sense of style and appropriateness, but the style and appropriateness of church members, both peers and parents. For the most part, female MCs must never show any cleavage and dresses can't be too short (by everyone's standards). If there are piercings, there can't be more than one per ear. Tattoos are completely taboo. When wearing a swim suit, only one piece swim suites are suitable and acceptable for female MCs. Even then, they must be very modest. Hair styles are expected to be "normal" according to the particular church and must not be viewed as radical by any church member. Male MCs don't have to worry about what they wear as much, but they are expected to follow certain rules: no tattoos, piercings or abnormal hair styles. Both male and female MCs are expected to be models of conservative dress. This is a very hard situation for teenagers to understand. They didn't sign up for this; they were born into it.

This is not the end of the typical Sunday morning for a minster's family. At the end of the service, the pastor usually has people that insist on talking to him about the most important things—some really are important and others are not important at all. So, the minister's wife has to reverse the entire process: take the children home, fix lunch and wait on the father to get home. Wow—what an impossible task. MCs must be dressed appropriately and behave perfectly at all times—in church, at home, while in public, shopping or playing. A pastor's wife and/or children showing up at church in less than the best clothes risk being judged unfairly. It is much easier to dress appropriately and avoid the comments, the stares and being the brunt of gossip.

QUESTIONS TO CONSIDER

For the Church Member

1. What ideas in this chapter caught you by surprise?

2. What situations do you remember your minister and their child being in that the normal church member would not encounter or experience?

3. Were there norms of behavior and dress that you imposed on your minister's children that were not fair or that were at a higher standard than children of church members?

4. What can you do to help a minister's wife on Sunday morning?

5. What can you do to help a minister ride home with his family after church on Sunday?

For the Minister

1. What can you do to change your Sunday morning routine in favor of your family?

CHAPTER FOUR
STEREOTYPES

"I don't stereotype, I profile."

The difference is a matter of perspective, and church members have their own perspective about everything and everyone, including MCs. The stereotypes of pastors' children are just that—stereotypes, and not true for most ministers' children. The stereotype that must be dispelled is that minister's children are bad or good. Being bad or good are extreme positions. For the most part, MCs are neither. They are, however, being exactly what they were created to be—individuals learning as they mature into responsible adults—individuals who will make mistakes in judgment as they learn. Yes, some seem to push the limits of morality, but most do not. Most of the MCs I have known were incredible Christian people. They were well respected by their peers and adults alike. They had a good reputation and were, for the most part, above reproach. In high school, they didn't party—as in drink, smoke, cuss, tell dirty jokes, have sex or even date—or have bad friends. Yes, there are a few that have tainted the rest, but this is not the norm. One MC said that when she was in 8th grade in PE, she said "one" cuss word. Before the day ended every student and adult in the school and church knew about it. Not only did they know about it, but so did her parents. And, to make matters worse, other students reminded her of it often throughout the remainder of middle school, high school and into college. She only cussed once and was never allowed to forget it. Any other student could cuss and others would care less, but not so if you are an MC. To combat this situation, MCs need a break. They will make mistakes. They will sin. They will disappoint others by their bad behavior. However, they are maturing into adults, and that is what teenagers do. I am not giving them a license to sin, but I am saying they need forgiveness and not to be reminded of their sin for the rest of their lives. To be sure, MCs need to strive very hard to take advantage of living in a clean home environment that is absent of much sin. The clean home environment of a MC should be seen as a huge advantage, instead of a prison to keep them from the world. Believe me; they will experience enough of the world when they get into the adult work-a-day world. They should cherish a clean, basically sin-free environment.

On another occasion the pastor's daughter got pregnant and got an abortion without her father or mother knowing. Her Sunday school teacher found out by accident and told her father, the pastor. Needless to say, the pastor was completely heartbroken and confused. He went through the normal stage of denial and disbelief. The pastor definitely had his confidence shaken. The situation almost cost the pastor his job and profession. On one hand, MCs are not responsible for their dad's success or lack thereof. However, as one MC said, we have no right to destroy his profession either.

It is easy to understand how an MC or any other child would think they are not part of his or her dad's job and a part of his success or failure. Pastors must be diligent as they raise their children to be beyond reproach and to have convictions about what they believe. It is not enough to give lip-service to what you believe. MCs must prove their belief with their actions. Those actions must include living a life that glorifies God. When this is done, the MC doesn't have to worry about behaving to save the image of their father. They are living for Christ, which is a much higher purpose and goal.

The Bible clearly states that a minister must rule his own house well. This is a qualification for being a minister. One can see how this scripture, well-known by church members, can be a huge mill stone around the father's neck. It is imperative that ministers not worry about saving the world unless they are being the father they have been called to be first. So, scripturally, an MC can put there their father's profession and calling in jeopardy. Churches place incredible responsibility on ministers to perform. By perform, most churches mean, grow the congregation numerically, be exciting, entertain them while discipling them and generally make them happy. Churches need to back off and let their ministers minister to their own families. There is the opposite stereo-type as well, the goody-two-shoes, never-do-anything-wrong, perfect-person-and-friend stereotype. The pressure placed upon MCs is immense. They are labeled by one action—right or wrong. Once labeled as "bad," most never recover. The expectations are so great that some stop trying and run away from the "good" label. Destroying the pressure of being a perfect teenager seems easy compared to living in fear of being found out. After all, we are all misbehavers. We all have weaknesses. Non-ministers' children can hide much of their bad behavior from the church in general. It is much harder for an MC to hide his or her bad behaviors.

My own children were labeled as "good" by church members, peers, school teachers, coaches and others. Because of this, they were not invited to parties, bonfires, trips, sleep-overs or camping trips where un-Christian behavior would be present. Other church members' children do not want the "pastor's child" to see them drink, smoke, cuss and be involved in behaviors deemed inappropriate for any Christian, whether adult or not. Most church members don't want their minister to know about their bad behavior. They play a game of hide and seek with their behavior with the pastor and his children. Yes, many MCs figure this out and see the hypocrisy of many church going teenagers at school and away from church. Being a pastor's child can be lonely.

Sometimes MCs are unfairly picked on or dismissed because their dads are ministers. Teachers and coaches, especially those who are unbelievers or who have different political views or morals, think the minister's child is an easy target. MCs should not take heat from teachers because of who they are. I think a certain amount is unavoidable. Pastors should be a little more sensitive to the pressures on their children and really nail people who mess with them, of course, in a Christ-like way! Every other child can write a paper on his or her dad's job or what their father's research and study has found. If an MC writes a paper on it, they may get told the paper is not acceptable or does not cover a "real" topic. This is very upsetting to the MC and the minister. It is also not very tolerant and is very bigoted.

The typical stereotype of ministers' children views teenagers as drinking, cussing, doing drugs, having sex and having the same behaviors as their non-Christian high school friends. This stereotype is not generally the rule, but rather the exception. The MCs that have great reputations are not heard from and fly under the radar. They are solid students that are well respected for who they are and not for who their father is or isn't.

Consider this excerpt from an article on a pastor's child that died from an overdose: "The death of Jon, son of _____, from an accidental overdose of drugs and drink, is one more example of that running tragedy; the troubled children of pastors....some pastor's children have turned to drugs as an escape or in attempt to seek their own identity. Some of them took their own lives. No matter how much love and attention, not to mention possessions, are heaped on the minister's children, many of them feel personally second-rate when compared to their fathers."
It seems impossible for them to measure up.

Every day of a MCs life, they have to contend with this, with even supposedly responsible people lumping them together as narrow minded, bigoted, moral police with failures of their own. Can you imagine reading those descriptions of what your life should be like? Can you imagine how it feels to know that this is the opinion of many people—strangers—have? That church members will accept gossip as true and that there is no way to fight it, no way to say, "That is not me. That is not who I am"? When your dad is a public person, you learn that if you have a problem, your problem is private and not to be told to anyone outside the family. Several students expressed a certain paranoia caused by so much of their families' lives, thoughts and actions being known by church members. It is kind of weird to have people walk into a room and know everything about your life and your family, but for you to know nothing about them.

One adult child of a minister was heard saying, "My dad was at every function physically, yet a million miles away mentally. Sometimes when he was making an effort to totally be there with me at my event, people were constantly distracting him with questions about their problems, life, ministry and the church. To the person it was only one question. To us it was a series of questions lasting all night long, many of which he would need to follow up on when we got home."

It is particularly unfair when they are asked to state their father's opinion about something on which he must remain impartial, like political candidates seeking election or issues in the church—whether to build a building or not, what color the carpet should be (some church members are sneaky and ask "what is your father's favorite color?"), does he like the new staff member, etc. There are even people who go so far as to accuse MCs of lying when they explain that he doesn't discuss his views with his family. It is like the child of a minister is living in an artificial environment called church and the minister's home. They are artificial because they do not mimic real life circumstances. In real life, people live out their sinful whims. In the church, people hide their sinful whims. In the pastor's home, life is lived as unto the Lord. Usually, this means MCs are raised in a sterile environment. I am not saying a sterile environment is bad. But one can see why it can be a difficult transition when an MC enters college and is exposed to a completely unfiltered world. In the artificial environments of the church and MC home, the MC rarely sees people lie, smoke, cuss, tell dirty jokes, drink, argue with their wife, scold their children, drive over the speed limit, not use their seatbelt, etc. When people, church and non-church members, find out they are in the presence of a minister or an MC, they clean up their behavior.

As a minister, it was hard to watch as my children were left out. But there was a part of me that was very proud of their Christian reputation. I pray most of their good behavior was more because what they thought of the Lord than me. After all, it is the Lord who is the ultimate person we want to please. My children spent most weekends at home. We didn't realize what was going on for a long time. But, then we would hear from other parents about parties, camping trips, and other events to which our children weren't invited. At some of those events, there was much unchristian behavior. I am glad our children missed that part of being a teenager. To offset these times of being uninvited and left out, ministers must have a full calendar of family events and outings scheduled so their children have a blast with their families.

Ministers need to model diligence when it comes to knowing their children's friends. Scripturally, we know without a doubt, that bad company corrupts good morals. As a minister, I was compelled to make sure our children had friends with good morals. We also found out an important part of raising teens is to know the friends of their friends—the third party friends. It is those third party friends that influence the friends of our children. We don't see where the influence is coming from, because we can't see it. It is not our child's friend that is cussing, but, rather the friend's friend that is cussing around our child. It is the friend's friend that slips the drugs to our child's friend, who then slips it to our child. All teens are influenced in this way with many behaviors. These behaviors usually blind-side a parent. For this reason, we found it important to know the friends of their friends. And, not only to know who the third party friends were, but who were their parents as well. Usually, it is these parents that don't mind if their children smoke and drink, as long as it is responsibly. Sometimes these friends of friends are simply the friend's older sibling or cousin. Ministers and all parents need to be diligent to know the friends of their children, and the friend's friends and family.

It is important for teens and parents to have a long range view of childhood friends. High school friends rarely last, yet teenagers put such energy and focus on friends, even to the detriment of their own family. The family will be there long-term, not teen friends.

A very important part of being an MC, and one that is not considered by non-minister parents and teenagers is that MCs must be selective about who they let connect to them. It is also important for MCs to gather together where they feel safe and affirmed. One MC said, "It is only among other pastor's children that we can relax and know no one will ask, "What's it like to be an minister's child?" This is also true of many other public professionals' children such as politicians, sports stars, famous actors, famous singers, etc.

Church members have admitted to being intimidated or at least hesitant to teach, disciple, and or mentor the minister's children. Church members think MCs know the Bible better than they, know all the answers, know correct teaching techniques and know how to pray, as if they are mature, professional, seminary-trained church ministers. In other professions, children are not set on the same pedestal as their professional parent. The child of an engineer, accountant or doctor is not thought to have the knowledge and skill of their parent. Yet, MCs have to deal with this on a regular basis. Peers and Bible teachers assume the MC knows facts, theology and doctrine and that they have memorized the maps and every person in the Bible. Not only is the teacher intimidated, but the other students in the group look to the minister's child to be the first to raise their hand and give the correct answer. To combat this situation, some MCs purposely withhold information, answers and getting involved in class discussion.

Spiritual Water-boarding

Ministers want their children to be Christians who love the church. However, they have to strike a balance when it comes to how much "church" is too much. Other children get to skip church once in a while and stay home. Other children go on vacation beginning or including

Sunday. Pastors don't have this luxury. They are expected to be in church, even when they are on vacation. Minister's families are expected to not only listen to every sermon, be ready for every Sunday School lesson and live perfect lives, but also to do morning devotionals which include prayer, Bible reading, and journaling. The question is, "When is too much "church" simply too much. For MCs it is like being strapped to a board and whether you want it or not, you are going to get some spiritual water – "water of life." Before you can take a breath and reflect on what you just heard or learned, you are getting more spiritual water. It is almost like you can't think or act fast enough before more information comes your way. It truly is like spiritual water-boarding. Everyone needs time to reflect and to have a little down time spiritually. I am not saying one can get too much Bible or Christianity. I am saying that if a minister continually dumps spirituality on their children, sooner or later, the child will throw up their hands and say "Enough, stop! I can't take anymore. I need to breathe!" As is the case in life, we need balance. Too much is simply too much. Too little is simply too little. Each MC has their own limits on how much they can take before needing a break.

Scripture clearly states that "it is the heart that is desperately wicked," (Jeremiah 17:9). All parents must focus on helping their children tame their heart. Mature parents will tell you it is not the amount of church attendance or Scripture memorized but rather if the child can tame their own heart. Does the child know that their own heart is desperately wicked and they are not immune to sin, if they put themselves in situations where they are going to be tempted and fall? They have to be taught how to overcome temptation and how to avoid temptation, when possible. At some point, the child must decide for themselves who their friends will be, and what they allow to influence them.

The Go-Between

Many MCs are caught in situations of being the communicator between a congregant and their dad, the minister. The church member will tell the MC to please tell their dad something for them. MCs get tired of members telling them to tell their dad to preach shorter sermons, for his choir to sing this song or that, for their dad to make sure more hymns are sung, as if the MC is the official go-between. For this situation to stop, the minister or the child must take the lead and tell people they will not tell their dad anything. If the church member wants to tell the minister something, they need to tell him themselves. This puts the child in the position of having to take control of the situation in which they have been placed. The minister won't always be around to coach congregants to communicate directly to him, so the MC will need to learn how to respectfully tell church members to tell their dad directly or joke that they never tell their dad anything church members say. In what other profession do children get to listen to church members talk (good and bad) about their dad. Many times church members talk about the minister in front of the MC like the MC isn't standing there listening. In what other professions do those being led attempt to communicate to the leader through the leader's children? In the corporate world, employees may not respect their boss, but they would never say bad things about him in front of their boss's children. MCs are intimately involved in their dad's ministry. Not many professions are involved quite like this. The perception in the church is that the minister works for the church members and the church members have a right to tell him how to raise his children. Without getting preachy here, the pastor ministers for God while leading a church. The pastor and his wife are the MCs parents, not the church.

QUESTIONS TO CONSIDER

For the Minister

1. Have you coached your congregation on how to respect you as a parent?

2. Have you coached your congregation how to communicate directly to you and to not use your child or wife as a communication conduit?

3. Have you placed your children, wife and family in general on your calendar first?

4. Who are your child's friends? Who are your child's friend's friends (third party friends)?

For the Church Member

1. Have you stereo-typed minister's children?

2. Do you value your pastor having a stable family more than the church growing? Are you willing to take on a ministry position in the church so the pastor can have the kind of family you expect?

3. What traits do you want your MCs to have?

4. Have you noticed your own children not inviting MCs to parties or outings? Why do you think they do this?

5. Who are your child's friends? Who are your child's friend's friends (third party friends)?

6. What behaviors do you hide from your minister(s)?

7. In what areas have you seen MCs used as the go-between or line of communication between a church member and minister?

CHAPTER FIVE
THE MINISTER'S JOB AND ITS EFFECT ON HIS CHILDREN

It was reassuring to find that most of the MCs I interviewed liked their dad's profession as well as his sermons, books and articles. They saw their dad's job and ministry as valuable and very important. It is also interesting to know they didn't read all their dad's books, or articles or watch their dad on TV—at least not much. There were exceptions, based on their dad's performance or leadership of the church in general, that raised issues for the children. The children had little or no way to correct these two problems. What if dad was not a very good speaker or is not a gifted leader? Other children and families have the opportunity to move to another church if the current pastor has these problems. What does the family of the pastor do when it is their father that is a bad preacher or leads the church to make bad administrative or financial decisions? What do they do when he is not a good pulpiteer or leader? The mom can't gather up the children and go to another church. If the pastor is not a gifted leader, this causes problems for the family as well because they may be moving...again.

"It is a lot of pressure to know that your behavior will affect your dad's job," said one MC. Being in a difficult situation is normal for MCs. If they behave, their dad may get to stay at the church and the MC gets to stay in school and on teams with friends and may not have to move to yet another town and school. If an MC misbehaves, they may have to move and lose friends, start over in sports and learn a new town. This may seem exciting and adventurous to those that have lived in the same town and attended the same church and school their entire lives. But for those who have to move often because of their father's profession, it is seen as having one's life turned upside down and beginning again.

It is an amazing revelation to know your dad is a man of God. With all of his faults, opinions and strengths, he really is a man that has been called by the Creator of the universe for a special purpose—to serve and lead the bride of Christ, the church. Other children may know their dad is a good Christian, but they never quite get the feeling in their spirit that their dad is a man of God, as in called out, separated, ordained and licensed into a life of ministry. To this end, it means the children of ministers are called to be a child of a minister. The children are not called to be a minister, though. Yet, many times they are treated and have the same expectations placed on them that are placed on their fathers. In the same way, it is up to each individual to accept Christ and follow His teachings. Sometimes, even with perfect parenting, MCs can choose a different path. Scripture teaches that if a child is brought up in the way they should go, they will not depart from it. This begs the question—In what way was the child brought up? Was the child shown one way at church and another at home?

There seems to be no formula for raising Godly children, but when a right spirit is combined with right actions, more times than not, children imitate their parents actions more than their teachings. Sometimes parents can do everything right. They present right teachings, set the right example by how they live, control outside influences, and involve the child in church, church activities, ministry and mission trips, yet, the child decides to forge their own path. The path may go in several directions. If the path involves behaviors that are disagreeable with church members, the pastor may be asked to resign. This is not fair to the father or mother or siblings. This begs the question, what is the age of accountability for a minister's child? At what age should the child be responsible for themselves? At what age should the minister be held accountable for the actions of their child? Answering these questions is not the purpose of this book. There are many variables when dealing with this issue. I have never been wrong when leaning on the side of grace towards parents with misbehaving children. Pastors need grace in this area as well. This brings us to the next point.

Consistency in the Pulpit and Home

Pastors preach and teach some lofty morals and behaviors and are expected to adhere to what they preach—at church and at home. A major problem can occur in a minster's family if there is no consistency. Ministers cannot make rules for their children and different rules for themselves. Ministers and their wives must live lives of complete integrity. They can't preach one thing and do the opposite. By living a life of integrity, the minister shows their children that they can live a life of confidence in who they are and have no need to pretend who they are or not. The children live a life of integrity as well. This is, after all, what is expected from church members, and more importantly from God. For example, a minister preaches against cussing and bad language in movies, and then uses bad language at home. And, you know, you can't do that. Particularly since the overall life is so unreal anyway. MCs grow up in homes where there is no cussing, telling of dirty jokes or even off color jokes, the watching of R-rated movies, an influence of alcohol or where their parents friends do these things in front of the minister or his children. If there are morals and rules for behavior as a Christian, those rules must be followed in the minister's home. Dad cannot preach against or for behaviors or attitudes and do the opposite in the home. Although this is accepted as a common practice among congregants, it is not allowed by ministers. Ministers must lead consistent lives both in and out of the church, both in and away from the home. Inconsistent behavior and beliefs confuse MCs. One MC was a very gifted athlete, as was his father. His father was a former Olympian and knew the sport. The MCs father provided steroids for his son, who won state titles. Later, it was discovered that steroids were involved and the state titles were taken away. Needless to say, this was not a good testimony. The father was able to keep his involvement from becoming public, while his son had his state titles stripped. The father was so consumed with protecting his own reputation and job that he left his son to fend for himself. The son and father have hardly spoken since. Yes, ministers can be out of balance and can be very competitive, as was this father.

Sometimes the minister is the cheerful, accommodating, listening, negotiating, team player at church. He gives everyone the time they want and expect. But at home he is different towards his family—not fun, stiff, has to have it his way, too busy to listen and does not have enough time for his family. Some MCs can't handle this and rebel against the inconsistency.

Time

The family should always come first. One can be deeply committed to family, calling and career without either suffering. On the other hand, MCs grow up accepting last-minute changes in plans—the possibility of having to postpone the family vacation or come back early because of an untimely death and funeral of a church member. At least it is untimely as far as the minister's family vacation is concerned. Other families only have to worry about the death of their own family and close friends. The minister's family has to be ready to plan around the deaths of every person in the congregation. They also have to plan around every wedding. Church members do not comprehend how much time this takes the pastor away from his family. No amount of scheduling by the minister can help him avoid these situations.

MCs find it very annoying and hard to accept that on the backside of nowhere they still may not be assured of an uninterrupted talk or of time alone together with their father or family. One would think that church members would realize, though they don't, when and where to talk to their minister and when and where to leave the family alone. For example, I was at a restaurant in Lynchburg, Va., eating lunch. One of the Vice Presidents of Liberty University came into the restaurant with his wife. Obviously, they were out together for lunch. It was also obvious that this was a time to leave them alone. I simply gave a polite nod of acknowledgment and left them alone. Church members need to do the same for their ministers. When ministers are eating a meal out with their family, it is family time. This is one of those times that church members need to give a polite nod of acknowledgement and move on. On the other hand, some pastors think they need to "work" every room whether it is the worship center or a restaurant. They leave their family sitting in the restaurant booth to spend time with a church family. Although this may be a nice gesture, pastors need to realize their family needs them more. It is the culmination of many situations like this that poison the heart of MCs. After seeing this happen over and over again, the MC simply says it happens all the time. After all, a minister is not seeking re-election like a politician. The minister stays at a church until God tells him to serve elsewhere. There is no need for the pastor to act like a president collecting support for an election.

The lack of time spent together is one of the hardships of having a successful parent in any profession, but, in most cases, the children and parents will agree that there are ways to compensate. Although loyalty to the family should be unquestioned, many MCs deny the high road and submit to rebellion and destruction and shatter the family. When a minister has a period of time when he is an absentee dad, the children must find ways to deal with it. MCs should never feel like they are playing second fiddle to their dad, the minister or the church. But, they do miss his presence. MCs understand how their family is different. It is important for parents to help their children see the strengths and weaknesses of their particular family and work to limit the weaknesses. All children want to see their parents grow as individuals, achieve goals and be successful.

An MC who is now a minister sat in my office and told about a time when his father was not there. The MC was a junior in high school and had worked hard to be a starter on the baseball team. One particular game, his team was losing by two runs in the ninth inning. The MC stepped up to the plate and hit a home run which allowed his team to win the game. The MC hit the winning walk-off home run!!! The MC then got very somber and began to choke back the tears as he told me how his dad wasn't there because he was visiting sick people in the hospital. Later, the dad said, he could have made the visits the next day and been at the game. Church members expect their pastor to visit every sick person in every hospital every day—with no exceptions. But, in the wake of these expectations is an MC that even after 20 years, chokes up as he recalls how he felt when his dad missed his greatest moment. Ministers need to plan hospital visits around their family extra-curricular activities.

Do MCs have ways of compensating for the lack of time together with their father? Not really. Sometimes they feel neglected—whether it is anyone's fault or not. Sometimes the MC withdraws. They get tired of dealing with all that goes with being the child of a minister. In some ways they feel very alienated. Dealing with it all the time causes family members to deal with it in different ways, depending on their personality. Being an MC alienates them from the outside world—from the real world. Not living in the real world isn't bad, it's just not real. You know, if you've been treated like a king for thirty years, eventually you're going to pick up the crown and stick it on your own head—whether it fits or not. In the same way, when your father and family have been beat up for 30 years, eventually you are going to get bitter, defensive and withdrawn from the group doing the beating. It is hard to find value in oneself when you and your family have been beat down for years.

As MCs become older, some ministers take their children on ministry and mission trips they think would be interesting for their child. A minister may be speaking at a youth camp and think it would be great for their child to be there. For the child, it is great to be at a youth camp, but it was just being with their father that they really enjoyed. Sometimes in their efforts to entertain their children, ministers forget how precious just being in their company is. Some of the most precious memories of fathers were those rare occasions when children have their fathers all to themselves—going out for lunch, Christmas shopping for Mom, a walk on the beach, just the two of them on the lake fishing. The times together as a family are special, too, from earliest memories of him sitting through extra-long childhood meals in the kitchen, making weird noises to distract the children from the horrible vegetables being cajoled into their mouths, to their most recent family evenings, playing cards, dominos, putting together a puzzle, talking and laughing together. Bedtime stories are some of the most precious memories we have as a family. It was time for just myself and our children to be together all to ourselves. These times were very special.

Pastor's children want to be proud of their dads and hear sermons that help them grow as a person and a Christian. They want to be able to brag on how well their dads preach. They never want to be embarrassed if their dad preaches a bad sermon or by being called out in front of a sanctuary full of people. One MC recalls sitting in church with his buddies. All of them were not paying attention and cutting up to the point of disrupting others. The MC was not the ring leader or doing anything more than the other boys. However, his dad called him out by name in front of everyone. This not only happens between ministers and their children; it happens between lay church members and MCs. An MC can be in the general vicinity of a group of misbehaving students, and it is the MC that gets in trouble. This is very unfair. Ministers need to be careful with this situation and make sure they talk to and discipline their child as they would any other child in the church. No minister would call out a church member's child during a service. The minister should not do it to his child either.

I had a guest evangelist come to our church to preach for a week. There had been a teenage girl in our church struggling with an eating disorder, and her mom wanted the evangelist, our pastor and me to pray over her at the conclusion of the service. I told my wife that I would be staying after the service to pray with the girl so she would not be waiting for me and could take our children home. After the end of the service, commitment time and saying goodbye to those wanting to talk after the service, we gathered to pray with the girl. As we were kneeling to pray, my wife came to me and said my six year old son needed to talk to me. She didn't say why. I reminded her about praying with the girl and said I would be home in a little while to talk with him. After we prayed for the girl, I went home. When I got home, I discovered the reason my six year old son wanted to talk. He had made a decision for Christ that night and wanted to talk to me specifically and pray to give his life to Christ. My heart went into my shoes—I was completely heartbroken. The joy of any father's life is to lead his own children to Christ, and I had completely missed it. This has been a sore spot in our relationship ever since. Although we have cried together and I have asked for and received forgiveness, we still struggle with this. I have apologized a million times, but it does not get rid of the lump in my throat if I allow myself to think about it. Yes, there was a victory that night. The girl we prayed over stopped having an eating disorder and later graduated from seminary and is helping other girls to this day. Personally, this may seem selfish because I would have rather spent time with my son when he asked and had the privilege to introduce him to Christ. Our church members never knew about this. It was not their fault…it just happened. I wish I had this time back!

Later in life many MCs realize their parents are getting older. This means that no matter how successful their dad was, nor how many lives he touched or led to the Lord, the new church members don't have the same vantage point as the MC. The MC has seen the sacrifices their dad has made, the late nights and early mornings. The shortened vacations, the missed ball games and piano recitals.

Older MCs realize they aren't always going to get to be with their dad, and they regret the times they didn't get along with him. There are times when the MC feels a little guilty for the times they could have gotten along with their parent(s). Here is one story from a father/daughter experience. "One night at dinner Dad was saying something about how he always wanted to take me on a month long mission trip to Africa, to go on a safari and to scale Kilimanjaro with me. (Yes, really to the top). And it never happened. Why didn't it happen? I was in my teens and wanted my freedom and arguing instead. To think I could've been doing things like that instead of being rebellious. As I look back on my teens, I realize my rebellion was not the fault of my parent(s). I did it all on my own from my limited perspective on life."

There are times when MCs are jealous of church members. Their dads are away at church or visiting members, doing funerals and weddings, counseling people and speaking to groups or at functions. Most pastors really love their family time, but they have difficulty balancing the two. The minister must always sway the balance of his time, energy and attention towards his family. If there has to be imbalance, the family must come out on top. It is especially hard for ministers when they don't really have one boss to whom they answer. Ministers answer to every church member, the deacons, the elders, etc. Many times, if they please one group, they displease the other. Ministers are stuck in a precarious position. This position is usually the cause of ministers making poor decisions about spending time with their families instead of doing "church work." There is a big difference between doing "church work" and the Lord's work. The MCs I talked to don't mind their father doing the Lord's work, however, they get tired of the church work.

Sometimes ministers and their families want to go out and eat a meal at a restaurant and not be bothered. Finally, you are doing something together as a family. You are spending time with him, and then all of a sudden it happens; Some well-meaning church member begins talking to the minister and telling stories. The minister's family is polite and gracious, but wishes the church member would leave. And, yes, on occasion, the church member will ask if they can join the family.

Church members appear to feel in some way they have a right to the time and attention of their pastor, and to some extent, they may be justified. The MC can find it hard to understand that the church member has a right to their dad's time. It is easy to understand the MCs jealousy toward the church member. The member's possessiveness is in direct conflict with the child's sense of ownership of his or her parents.

Street Smarts

Some MCs never learn the 'street smarts' that helped their parents be successful. The parent comes from a background and learned street smarts to survive and get ahead—that is, unorthodox means of self-preservation—to help them be successful. We would all rather depend on the wisdom of God than street smarts, or as the Bible states it, "our own understanding, Proverbs 3:5-6." Sometimes when a parent comes from one of these hard "street" environments, they make sure their children never have to deal with the same environment. The parents overprotect the child; they take care of their every need. Then when the child gets out into the world, he's defenseless. He becomes a victim. The people around him pick him to pieces because he does not have any street smarts. It is almost like they are too trusting of those around them. They haven't learned how to discern people's intentions. They take people at their word. It doesn't take long for them to learn how the world really works. It happens to a lot of MCs. MCs should not be isolated from the world as if that will keep them innocent and away from evil. The Bible says, "the heart is desperately wicked," (Jeremiah 17:9). One cannot only worry about outside influences, but it is important to focus on the heart as well. All people are different with different personalities, wants and needs and should be treated as such. It is the heart that needs to be the focus of parents and eventually, the focus of the MC. It is not wise to only focus on outside influences. There is a balance between keeping children innocent as long as possible (once innocence is lost, it is gone forever). MCs should however, be raised in the best atmosphere possible. MCs can't be reared based on the multiple perspectives of a church full of people or by what church members think or say. MCs must follow God.

Even Jesus had time in the wilderness. He had to make up his mind to depend on God's Word or listen to what seemed to be reason from a very unreliable source – Satan.

Spiritual War

This seems to be a recurring theme, that is, that MCs deal with things that others don't. All ministers and missionaries will tell you the spiritual attacks are real. Ministers and their families have targets on their backs, and Satan loves to shoot at them, harass them, and does his best to kill, steal and destroy the minister, his family, his joy, ministry and future. This subject deserves an entire book, but we will let the testimony of an MC say it all. "And when we came home, we came under extreme spiritual attack at home. We were all tired and we just wanted to rest and this is what we got instead of resting. I could also feel that attack inside of me, and I've never felt anything like this before. We got together to pray and it was wonderful how our great God showed us His power and defended us. The pastor and his family come under a lot of spiritual attack because it's a huge victory for the Devil if he wins over God's servant. I learned that there's no resting in the fight for spirits."

The Pastor's Image and Respect

One MC said, "I used to resent my dad keeping me respectable because of his image, rather than because he loved me. Now, these many years later, I know it was because he loved me." Sometimes MCs may think their dad's image placed unfair expectations on them. It is hard for the MC to know if it was his concern with if he was respected or church member's concern with his image and being respected in the community. It is important for a minister to have a good image. Since there is Scripture saying a minister's child should be respectable, MCs are held to this standard. However, if Scriptures are examined more closely, many examples are found of MCs behaving badly. An Old Testament MC would be the son or daughter of a prophet or priest or king. There is one simple fact---each person is autonomous and has to respond to Christ, work out their faith and make it his or her own. We can't ride into heaven on the faith of our parents. The minister is supposed to lead his home and family, but not in a heavy handed, demanding, autocratic way.

Their father's image and the respect he garners in the community on behalf of the church is a big deal. It affects the self-image of the pastor, his wife and their children. MCs want their dad to have a positive image. It helps them have a reputation as someone with credibility and integrity, a person raised in an all-American family. Hopefully, this gives the MC an advantage when meeting someone for the first time, as they may receive the benefit of the doubt. The reasoning goes something like this— if people think positively about your dad, maybe they will think positively about you. It is nice when you meet someone for the first time and they accept you as they would your father. It is also a good feeling to know that when someone meets your dad at the grocery store, they will, for the most part, tell the rest of their family or friends they ran into your dad. If the father has a good image and reputation and is respected, then being in public with him can be nice. It is wonderful when people meet an MC for the first time and have some kind of feeling that something nice happened in their day, and they're going to go home and tell their wife and children that they met the son or daughter of.… You've got them on your side. This is a very nice feeling.

Children also mirror their parents. They're expected to be a certain way, and most don't want to do anything to embarrass their father, especially if they are in a close circle of his friends or peers. An MC not only lets down their family, but all of the close family friends from the church. It is a scary thing when a child either does not care about those around them, or they are so caught up with themselves that they place themselves above others. To engage in destructive behaviors is not good, whether you are an MC or not. Just because you are an MC does not give you permission to destroy your life and the image of those around you. There have been many ministers fired because their child was out of control. One MC said, "As a pastor's kid there are a lot of expectation for us, but I think personally, in our church, I ruined their expectations so they don't have much left for me, and I like it better."

Parents (the minister and his wife) should never suggest that their child's behavior should be influenced by Dad's reputation or image. The pressure that is felt to perform a certain way, to play it straight and be sure not to cause any shame, should come from within and be motivated by the love of the Lord. That is not to say that MCs are allowed to act any way they want until they get ready to behave right. As in most things, there has to be a balance.

On the contrary, one father pointed it out to his children that they behave a certain way by using phrases such as, "What happens if someone sees you doing that as the preacher's child?" or "You really shouldn't do that because it will look bad on me." Eventually MCs may begin to believe him. At first you may blow your parent off and want to do what you want. Then you will realize that it's really true, that it can hinder his ministry, and he has worked really hard to be successful. Who are you to destroy or derail it? Some MCs participate in bad behavior in public when they are immature. Then they get to deal with the congregants and their parents. When they become older, they become more discrete and even private so their bad behavior doesn't attract attention. They learn quickly it is easier to rebel in private and away from church members. This is one reason MCs find friends whose parents have no connection to the church. Some MCs gravitate to these type of friends simply because they are not judged and can be exactly who they want to be and do what they want to do. Most MCs don't want a bad reputation; they just want to escape the focus by hiding in the fishbowl. Usually, after a few years of living up to their father's reputation and the expectations that go with it, of trying either to prove or deny their father really is a man of God, they finally learned simply to accept it—to accept people's reactions to it. Some MCs find it hard to sit down and really talk about how difficult it is to be an MC, and others love talking about it.

Some MCs engage in behavior that embarrasses their parents. One child flipped their dad's truck one night and came home drunk. Everybody in the church knew what the MC had done. Another MC got caught trespassing, stealing, outrunning cops and having to get bailed out of jail. Afterward, the child was more embarrassed than the father. The MC can't believe they were involved in that behavior. And, they can't believe they have to deal with the long-term consequences of such behavior.

One MC said, "I always used to feel I would never be as popular and smart as my dad. Most children learn it is best to be who they are and not compare their level of intelligence to their parents. But, when your dad is supposed to have the correct biblical and spiritual answer to all of life's problems, it can be overwhelming. After all, your dad has the wisdom of God from which to draw. Surely he is right? Wrong! As is the case with most fathers, ministers do the best they can and understand they fail a lot as a parent and as a minister. MCs must understand and accept this as well and love their fathers anyway.

It is nice to be a pastor, but after years of loving people and serving them, when you are ready to retire, are slowing down or they don't want you anymore, it's nice to have a family to turn to and lean on, to reminisce with, and not end up an empty person. This is a reality many MCs see when their dad is nearing retirement. His preaching is not as sharp, he is not as contemporary as he once was and he is not as energetic. When this happens, churches are ready to move on to the next minister. Yes, most appreciate his effort, heart for God and tireless pursuit of being a Godly example. This too, is a hard reality for MCs, for MCs have seen their dad's ministry over 40 years at every church. They have seen their dad grow spiritually and personally. They have seen the multitudes that have been helped by their dad and the sacrifices their dad has made on their behalf. MCs also understand the sacrifices the entire family has made for the church. This is different for a church that only sees what a minister does at one church for a few years. The MC takes on the feelings of his or her father, because he or she has lived through his career as a minister.

QUESTIONS TO CONSIDER

For the Minister

1. Can you separate your father's calling from your Christianity or spiritual maturity?

2. In what ways are you consistent and inconsistent with your beliefs and behaviors as a minister? As a minister's child?

3. Is your first priority your wife and children? What is your children's answer to this question? What is your wife's answer to this question?

CHAPTER SIX
TO FOLLOW OR NOT TO FOLLOW DAD INTO THE MINISTRY—THAT IS THE QUESTION FOR ME!

▼

What about following your dad into ministry? MCs spend years hearing half-truths and lies told about their fathers. They have experienced their father being forced out of or fired from a church. Most of the time their fathers were fired based on a few members not liking their father. These few people gossip and spin their stories to gain support from a majority of the church members. Then these disgruntled church members, with supporters in tow, have the pastor removed. They have seen their fathers attacked because they took a stand on issues that are 100 percent biblical. Sometimes when a pastor makes small changes in the church, they are attacked. It is as if everything is sacred and one dare not remove or change anything–even the 50-year-old carpet. Politicians are not the only spin-masters in the world. As one MC said, "I have heard and seen all the church stuff. I didn't want to go through that stuff over and over again." Any individual would struggle with going into a job where they know they will get beat up emotionally, spiritually and relationally. The difference with becoming a pastor is that you don't really have a choice to follow God's will for your life or not. It is a privilege to be asked by God to be His servant. The non-church going outsider may think it arrogant to think one is really called by God to serve Him in a special way. Church people know it to be a very humbling experience. So for the pastor's child, it is usually something he only runs from—not something he wakes up one day and says, "Hey! I think I will be a pastor!" However, when God calls MCs into ministry, they remember the things their fathers' struggles. Some accept the call anyway. Some try to use what their father went through to justify not going into ministry. Some do a good job of destroying their reputation and character so they would never be accepted by the church as a pastor. It is a struggle, at the least, to follow your dad into ministry. Many MCs spend years getting over or forgetting their father's unimaginable pain as a minister.

On the other hand, it makes a lot of sense whenever you hear about someone going off and doing something entirely on his own terms, unrelated, like being a fisherman in the North Sea or off the coast of Alaska; It is something different, and no one will ever compare you. Sometimes the comparisons are annoying, and sometimes they are flattering.

MCs want to be respected because of who they are as an individual separated from their father's image and reputation. Some MCs get away from places and people where these things become an issue. They want to get away from the whole thing and sort things out. Some spend a lifetime sorting it all out. On the other hand, who your father is, can be a huge blessing.

Why not take advantage of your dad's connections and influence, just as every other child would in any other profession? Again, this is normal. An MC will have plenty of time to establish themselves as a separate individual from their father and his ministry.

The topic arousing some of the most explosive reactions from the MCs I talked with was the idea of following in their parents' footsteps. Choosing a career is one of the most important decisions in life; When it turns into a calling from God, it gets even more complicated. It is like being put in double jeopardy. You want to follow God and accept His call into ministry, but at the same time you want to make sure you are not just following your father. When you are under the microscope of a church, you understand that conclusions will be drawn whatever you decide. It is not that people are talking about it and drawing wrong conclusions based on wrong assumptions. Conclusions are a funny thing and must be dismissed by MCs and ministers alike. For instance, if a minister's wife wears a suit, somebody will say she is dressing down or very conservatively or being a power player. On days when she wears a more light hearted dress or is casual—even if she is wearing what she is comfortable in—someone will say, "She is trying to compete with…" They will interpret whatever they want to interpret. So, when it comes to an MC being called into ministry, they have already learned to be thick skinned and dismiss the frivolity of the gossip chain.

What if you happen to have a father who is pastoring one of the largest churches in America. You, too, establish yourself as a great leader and your church becomes large as well. This isn't anything to complain about, right? Your father is a gifted leader, and so are you. You are doing it on your own, as your father did. If your mother and/or father are genuinely gifted and smart and industrious, what's the problem? Yet, some MCs accept a call from God into ministry, but want to make it on their own, to prove themselves without taking advantage of their parents' connections, experience and wisdom. If your father is a great football coach, and you hung around him in the film room, as he talked strategy and game planning, then naturally, you know a lot and have a base of knowledge from which to build your own coaching expertise. A great example fitting this situation is Archie Manning, former NFL quarterback of the New Orleans Saints, and his sons, Peyton and Eli. Peyton wanted to make his own way by not following in his father's cleats and playing football in Mississippi. Payton chose to play for the University of Tennessee Volunteers. This was seen by many people in Mississippi as being a traitor. On the other hand, Eli followed in his father's footsteps and played for his father's alma mater. He still had to perform to play, but he didn't mind the comparisons and borrowing on the good reputation of his father. If your father is a minister, you as an MC should use the wisdom and experience of your dad to be the best minister you can be. Isn't this natural? So, why do MCs struggle with this so much?

One young pastor was asked, "Do you think that the reason you chose being a minister as a career was to establish your own identity after living all your life as a pastor's child?" For some, it never occurred to them. As a minister's child you need to choose the career that fulfills every part of you—spiritual, intellectual, emotional and physical. Use *your* gifts and talents, not your father's. Create your own future that will allow you the opportunities you want. Ministers' children's career decisions could not have been uninfluenced by their fathers, but more importantly, their decisions were influenced directly by the kind of people their parents were. Can you fool yourself to think that your father's occupation and who he was hasn't affected you? If you become a minister, did you do it of your own free will? Or was it something that was around you your whole life? An MC has stated, "Am I making the decision as a free agent? I don't know, and I probably never will know. I hope it is because God has called me to it and no other reason."

There has to be a time when you pass a certain level of maturity that you have to say, 'I've decided this on my own, and I will be successful because of my talents and ability, not that of my father. I achieved it on my own.' Someone asked a minister's child, "You want to be a minister? For the rest of your life, people will compare you to your father." It can be a tremendous burden all of one's life to have the expectation, false or not, that perfection is the only standard. This can be especially hard in school and in front of friends. It is also this mantra that drives so many MCs to give up. They know they will never be perfect so they stop trying. Finally, when they are mature, they realize it was never about being perfect. It was about following the One who is perfect—Jesus Christ. It takes MCs time to figure out they don't have to be perfect. They just need to be who they were created to be.

MCs grow in their relationship to their father. Some, when they are young, feel inferior to their dads, because it seemed he knew everything and they didn't know anything. Grown MCs can actually sit with their father and have a discussion with him and feel that they are equal to him. It can be a bit intimidating when your father is looked up to as a fountain of knowledge and wisdom, whose every word is taken as gospel and as from God. Who wouldn't grow up feeling inferior? There is a painful moment in life when it is realized that parents are not infallible. But when your father is a minister, this common discovery takes on a proportion of crushing sacrilege. Maybe this is why many of the most successful pastors don't take themselves too seriously and have a great sense of humor and candor with others. They know fully the Scripture about the "foolishness of preaching" and know it is God that gives favor and increase. God did not give us a burden to carry; we load our own burden. Ministers and their families need to enjoy the journey.

Do you think that if you were to become a minister, people would put a little halo over your head that doesn't belong there? For sure, people do it all the time to ministers. Congregants have high expectations of ministers and their families. When we don't live up to their expectations, they tend to get bitter. It is hard to follow in your father's footsteps when he is a very successful pastor. Church members have the same expectations of you as they would of your father. They transfer the same expectations to you. Hopefully, you will never have to worry about letting your father down or anything like that. Your father doesn't ever want you, the MC, to let yourself down. The only way you will ever let your father down is by letting yourself down. He wants you to be who God has created you to be. Maybe God has gifted you to be a great pastor to small churches. That is not a bad thing, as long as it is a God thing. The only way a father should be disappointed is if you let yourself down; But he will still support you and be in your corner.

When an MC returns from college and seminary and begins working for their father in the church, it can have a great impact on their relationship. At that point, the MC is old enough and has a relationship with his father in which there is good communication. You can have a feeling that you could have a part in your father's ministry. Why would you walk away from a situation like that? Especially if you are called to be a minister as well, and your gifts compliment the work to which God has called your father.

QUESTIONS TO CONSIDER

For the Minister

1. Do you want your child to follow you into ministry? Why? Why Not?

2. Identify your child's negative experiences that would cause them to find another profession?

3. Has your child established their own identity in Christ?

For the Minister's Child

1. Do you want to follow your dad into ministry? Why? Why Not?

2. What negative experiences would cause you to find another profession?

3. Have you established your own identity separate from that of your father?

CHAPTER SEVEN
THE FAMILY CIRCUS
(OR SO IT SEEMS!)

"It is better to be unknown because of who you are, than to be known because of who you are not."[1] — *Arlo Guthrie*

Being an MC is weird in another way. As parents, we first noticed it when our children were young. Part of it was our desire for them to get along with their friends by being accommodating, selfless and simply a good friend. Our children would go over to a friend's house to play and generally have a good time. When our children would return home they would say, "All the other child wanted to do was play such-and-such, and I didn't want to do that at all." We, as parents, would say, "When you are at someone else's home, you need to be the guest and follow their lead and do what they want." This sounded right to us. After all, scripture says, "consider others before yourself," (Philippians 2:3). But the situation got complicated when our children would have friends come over to our house to play. The visiting friend wanted to do things that our children didn't want to do. When the friend left, we, as parents, would say, "When you are the host, you need to be accommodating and let them do the things here that they never get to do at home—like jump on the trampoline or play in the treehouse." It took us, as parents, a little while to realize what we were doing. We had placed our children in a no-win situation. Our children were never getting to do what they wanted. As the minister's child, they were never getting to do the things they wanted to do. Joy and I had to rethink our position. It is not always the other person that should get their way. At the same time, our children should not get their way all of the time either. There needs to be a balance, and just because our children's dad was the minister didn't give them the right to get their way. Neither should they have to always give up their "wants." We decided to show them how to negotiate so both got to do what they wanted. This helped them learn how to negotiate as adults. After all, adults don't get their way all the time either and need to have negotiation skills.

It is difficult for an MC to live two lives and have two identities. They don't do it on purpose, but it kind of evolves as they mature. They really just want to be themselves as a normal maturing teenager who has friends, goes on dates (or not), goes to school (gets good or bad grades) and gets married. As the conversation goes in their heads, "because I want to be me, not only my father's child. Although there is nothing wrong with being his child, I still need to be me. I am my father's daughter, who does not go on dates or wear bikinis or have a Facebook account or have a smart phone (and the list goes on). Maybe I am not that good in school yet not being rebellious. Does that count? Do I have to be like Mary Poppins and be perfect in every way? Where does being a pastor's child end and being me begin? I want people to see me apart from my father. It isn't that I don't like being associated with him. After all, I think he is an amazing man of God." The problem is that MCs try to find themselves, and congregations and friends continue to relate them to their father. It can be confusing.   Part of growing up is deciding who we want to be in Christ and the world and what actions to take or avoid in order to live up to that life. That learning and sifting process is complicated by also having to take into account what life our parents present to the world and whether we want to support, deny or destroy their life and their image.

When finally moved into a college dorm away from parents, many MCs have a chance to be themselves. Finally, for the MC, it is a chance to be themselves, to be liked or disliked based on their own being. I could talk about things like where I went to school and what kind of music I liked, instead of hearing, "Wow, how does your father feel about…? He must really… Do you get to…?"

Many MCs make no attempt to hide who their father is, but neither do they introduced themselves by saying, "Hi, I'm _____, and my father is _____ _____."

One of the toughest things for MCs is breaking down preconceived notions of who they are and what they should be. They have to be themselves, which is the easiest thing, and either they offend people or they don't. This is another complex situation with which they learn to live.

Teenagers are teenagers, whether they are pastor's children or not. One said of his life, "I was getting caught up with friends, school and extra-curricular activities and integrating un-clarified personal values as I went. Things got messy quickly. Part of it was my gratifying all these newly discovered areas of my life. After all, this is what my friends were doing." MCs cannot allow others to control friendships. MCs are similar to professional athletes or other popular figures that have to pick their friends. They cannot accept everyone who wants to be a friend. They have to be choosy.

Another simple example of image is that some MCs let their clothes define their attitude or who they are and how people look at them. People look at them and see their clothes and forget that there's somebody there. Clothes should accentuate who you are; you shouldn't have the clothes define your persona. The goal is to be who you are when you are with only family and you are just being yourself. You should not be one way around family, another around church members, and yet another way around friends. MCs should be exactly who they are in every situation.

As an MC, it's good to know what you want and to know it young. Pastors' children have to know what they want at a young age to avoid becoming confused as they try to live up to other people's expectations. MCs have a particularly striking reputation to live up to or to live down. There's probably no way they can behave that wouldn't confirm what some people expect. People aren't reacting to the MC, particularly. They are reacting to the actions or beliefs of the father's child. What people think about the MC is more of an indication of what they are like than what we are like. The

Bible states clearly that it is from the mouth that the heart speaks. This is another way of saying we mirror in others what we see in ourselves. This includes mirroring behavior, attitude, and motives. Rarely is the MC seen for whom they are but rather the mirror image of the observer. Thus the interpretation of the observer is wrong.

I think that the most valuable thing MCs can learn from both parents is that they are who they are, and the MC had to grow up, as hard as it was or as easy as it was, allowing the parents to be themselves as well. It is a hard fact to deal with, that you're a minister's child. The MC can make their life much harder than it should be. Every child of a minister faces it in one way or another; it's a question of how do you sift through it so it makes sense and does not destroy you. For example, if you happen to have a father who is a genius, and you are following in his footsteps, or if your mother and/or father are genuinely gifted and smart and industrious, why would you run away from their help and support. Yes, you want to be your own person, but you should also take advantage of their success.

A friend of mine dates a recognizable MCs son, and is well acquainted with that whole thing of being associated with someone who's famous, of going into a restaurant, and all the attention's on them. This friend has stated, "But, it must be pointed out, the difference is that if you are dating a famous person, you are there by choice. I cannot choose who my father is as a minister's child. He had his career long before he had me. I didn't choose to be in the situation."

Friendships

My children have had to let some friendships go when friends begin to be involved in un-Christian behavior. This is, perhaps, the hardest thing for any child. I say all this to say…they are normal children in every sense except they are the child of a minister.

Another common problem for minister's children is having too many or not enough friends. When arriving at a new church, all the children in the church close to the new MCs age are sizing up the new child(ren). At first, they all want to be their friend. They all see something they have in common and begin testing the waters of friendship. Over time it is discovered whether there is really much in common. The MC gravitates to a few close friends, not meaning to exclude any. However, it may not seem that way to the other children in the church. When first getting to a new church, the MC is invited to every activity by every student in the church. There are a few problems this creates. First, if there is more than one invitation to the same event or an event that is at the same time and date, who do you go with? Second, all of the events cost money. What if the parents simply can't afford for their child to go to all the events to which they are invited? If an invitation is declined does the MC say they already have something to do? If they do and they are seen out with someone else, sometimes the one whose invitation was rejected says, the MC prefers the other child. This is not the case at all, but maybe it is the case.

Some parents want their son or daughter to hang out with the new MC because they feel the MC will be a good influence on their child. MCs are not the fix-all relationship for dysfunctional children from the church. If ministers are not careful, their own children will have all the "messed up" children shoved at their children as friends. In most cases, the larger the church, the more people with problems will attend. Another way of saying it is, "The brighter the light, the more bugs you attract." Some churches do a great job of attracting hurting people and helping them come to terms with their sin, struggles and suffering and then accepting Christ as their Savior. This is, after all, the church's purpose. People with problems are not bugs, but humans created in God's image. I guess as a teenager, it may seem that these people were strange. In fact, they were needy and that is one of the reasons the church exists.

One MC explained, "One of my first boyfriends did not understand my father's beliefs. He really didn't understand. The first time I encountered this I really didn't know how to respond. I pretended to agree, and even talked myself into agreeing to be accepted. I went through a period of thinking my father beliefs were off base and out of touch. In reality, his beliefs were identical to my beliefs. It is just that his belief were maturely stated and supported. In fact, I liked his sermons and things he believed, but I went along with popular opinion. I feel differently now. It is embarrassing to think I felt that way. I was so conflicted. I wasn't trying to be rebellious as much as I wanted to be accepted by my peer group."

She continues to say, "In the last few years I've been very careful to make new friends who are positive and not degrading about my background or family, who are going to be supportive. Before, there were people in my life who were judgmental or critical of me, and I didn't realize that maybe they weren't the best people for me."

Another common problem is birthday parties and whom to invite. MCs are under pressure to invite everybody. If someone is not invited, they may feel like it was done on purpose with mean intentions. Again…this is not the case at all. MCs need to have the freedom to invite or not, whomever they want to their party. On the other hand, MCs are not invited to events where non-ministers' children will be involved in un-Christian behavior. Then on Sunday morning, the other children are talking about what a great time they had together. The MC feels left out—especially if he or she is the only one that was not invited.

One of the common complaints of minister's children is that they don't feel free to express their sometimes negative feelings about their parents, even to their peers, for fear of tarnishing the parent's image or ministry. There is pressure felt to keep up a front. A friend stated, "It is like we always have to be appropriate, say the appropriate thing, although what is going on in the MCs mind may not be appropriate at all. It is one thing to have character and another to be a character. We are not characters in a jar.

Dating is one of the hard circumstances to deal with for the MC. There are so many opinions about dating in the church. Do you date? Should you date? Whom do you date? At what age do you start dating? Can you date only church member's children? Should you date another church member's child at all? Will there be hard feelings when you break up? (And you will break up.) Then there are issues related to your dad about dating. Will others date you or not because your dad is the pastor? It is a very intense thing. People say MCs are over protected and spoiled, but it is an odd thing not being able to go on dates, swim in a bikini, wear certain clothes or shoes or eat in certain restaurants. MCs deal with plenty of complex situations. It is frustrating to go to a swim party and be the only girl there with a one piece swimsuit, like you are a Puritan. Or as if you believe that if a guy sees your skin he will completely lose his mind.

Popularity of the minister, especially if he is on TV or speaks or sings on the road for a living, can be hard on the family. For some high profile pastors and musicians it is harder. Church members and others who follow the minister on the radio or TV begin to treat the pastor like a celebrity and become a fan. Ministers aren't supposed to have fans; they are supposed to point everyone to Jesus as the ultimate person to follow. But people are also looking for those in which to believe. When they see the minister, and he seems like Mary Poppins, perfect in every way, they can get enamored and become fan-like.

Some "fans" stayed behind to meet and get the autograph of a popular pastor. The MC heard them say, 'Oh! I love you! I love you!' to which his child turned to his father and asked, "How can they love you? They don't even know you."

QUESTIONS TO CONSIDER

1. Do you act one way in front of church members and another way around your family or friends?

2. Do you feel pressure to live up to a certain image?

3. Are there ways of separating your image from that of your father's without engaging in self-destructive behavior or behaving like a non-Christian?

4. Have you made it more difficult than it had to be as an MC?

5. How do you handle the constant interruptions while in public with your dad?

6. To whom do you express your negative feelings about your father?

7. What are your true feelings about dating? How do your thoughts and feelings differ from that of your father? Differ from that of the current church?

8. Do you want to be accepted by your peers more than you want to be rebellious?

Bibliography

1. Arlo Guthrie: The Warner/Reprise Years, Hank Reineke, Scarecrow Press, 2012.

CHAPTER EIGHT
CHURCH AFFECTS

Some children feel they have to prove themselves to everybody. They have be perfect little Christians, have 100 percent Sunday school attendance, dress appropriately and generally fit into every church member's little minister's child box. Young children don't understand their father's lives very well at all. Close friends usually never make comments or think it is unusual if the MC is not perfect. One MC said, "It was always the people who weren't close to our family, who were not close to my father, [who] didn't know us as individuals that tried to hurt us by cutting down the character, leadership or sermons of our father." They will sometimes make comments like, "When is your father going to grow up and do something serious?" "Is that all they want to do with their life?" It is the insensitivity of well-meaning people that is most destructive to the children of pastors and staff of churches and that create and perpetuate the lack of discrete identity needed by MCs.

There are many questions that MCs get tired of answering. Wasn't it very difficult growing up as a minister's child? Didn't people always make a fuss about you at church? You can see them thinking, "Oh, okay, so you are the minister's child. I need to be careful about what I say." "Are you any relation to…? He seems like such a nice man—." "Is he really like that at home?" Sometimes MCs deny the relationship altogether because they just aren't in the mood to hear, "Oh, he's my favorite preacher!"

What do MCs think about their Sunday school teacher and others thinking they know every verse and have every right answer to every Sunday school question? Did people try to connect themselves to you relationally so their image would escalate among church members—you know—being the best friend of the pastor's child was huge.

Taking sides with different groups or being identified with them can be a problem as well. If they attend a certain party or function, it is assumed they completely agree with that group's position. If they don't outright come out against a group, it is assumed that they agree with them. For this reason and others, some MCs don't socialize a lot. They get weary of putting themselves in situations of being unfairly judged. When people come over, and the mother is vacuuming and the father is working the compost heap, little by little they realize that we all have to eat and go to the bathroom and sleep at night.

What kind of pressure is placed upon MCs? Church members are always curious about how a pastor really feels about different topics or issues. Often they'll ask, "Are you in political agreement with your dad?" One must be careful how they answer. It is best for the MCs to tell people to ask their dad these types of questions. At first many church leaders invite the MC to attend all the youth activities and ministries because they think they would draw other students. And it works. But if an MC is not a genuinely nice person, Christian and a charismatic leader, the other students won't follow them. Leaders always wanted the pastor's child to be at camp so other children would come. MCs are expected to be at all church related activities—every time the door is open. This is an unfair expectation. MCs should be given permission to miss activities from time to time.

Every other child in church can go to the restroom during the sermon. The minister's child must sit in misery because of what church members may think or say. When a minister's child goes to the restroom it is said of them, that they are setting a bad example for the rest of the children or that they have just given all the other children permission to go to the restroom. If the minister's child needs the restroom, they should be allowed to go. Just like other children, they need to adjust to the expectations of the general rules and not bow to the "extra" rules because they are MCs.

The viciousness with which certain church members attack ministers and their children is baffling. Each time a new piece of gossip is shared, after the rage has subsided, MCs are left wondering, "Why?" We are all aware of how words can be twisted—how description and commentary can make the most innocent incident sound ignoble. But why anyone would want to take this attitude will always be baffling. Once, an MC went to church in an antique dressing gown. Is it jealousy, or a mean spirit or some grudge against an MCs parents that would lead someone to describe a beautiful antique dressing gown as an "old ragged housecoat?" It may be another way of saying the same thing but with quite a different intent, and quite a different effect.

How do MCs deal with questions from church members? Some give no reply at all. Some do their best to be cautious and try not to make the situation worse. Sometimes, the MC does really want to say what is on his or her mind so people cannot put words in their mouths for them. Even when MCs say what is on their minds, they are often quoted out of context.

Pastors are wrongly accused of all kinds of things—even marital problems—by such delusional people. One church member asked a pastor's child "Is your dad seeing anyone?" Is your mother seeing anyone?" MCs must learn to dismiss these kinds of statements or to avoid situations where they may be questioned.

MCs do not always have to be tolerant of their dads' supporters (church members). Some days they just want to go to church and not be the pastor's child. They want to leave the church without everybody saying how much they liked the sermon. Or without hearing a story about their dad that they say the MC has probably already heard, but that they proceed to tell anyway, one more time. Or without hearing about how much they loved the illustration which they then proceed to retell. It gets hard to smile; it gets hard to be polite, to say, 'Oh thank you, great, super, I'll tell him you said so.'

One feels pressure to always smile and be polite, to say, "Oh, yes, yes … Well, I'll be sure to tell him…Yes, that's so nice of you." Sometimes MCs blush with pride, but some days they just are not in the mood to be gracious. Oh yes, MCs have to hear about the church member's favorite sermon or illustration (even if they get the illustration completely wrong) and have to say, "Oh thank you, thank you." It is so much trouble to argue with people who are going to insist they are right. After a while it doesn't bother MCs that much, because they realize they have to do it. Because they're dad's supporters, they support their dad's ministry. Most want to see you, too, and support you. This is a big joy in the life of an MC. Pastors' children are like public figures….they ARE public figures. They have no choice, and if it gives other people pleasure, what's the big deal?

Many pastors use their family members as sermon illustrations; MCs are constantly having their lives put on display and paraded in front of entire congregations. Their good, bad, goofy and awkward behaviors are announced from the pulpit for all to make judgments. Wise pastors refrain from this and at least keep their children anonymous when telling stories in which they were involved.

For most children, moving is a good experience because dad is getting a promotion. For many MCs they are leaving a church because their dad was forced out, and they have hard feelings toward the former church. Then they are expected to embrace a new church even though they are still dealing with the old feelings. My daughter had an experience when moving to a new church that was very difficult. At the previous church, all the students sat in the first few rows near the front of the church. They had a blast sitting together and usually weren't too distracting. They loved to pull pranks on other students. One prank was when everyone stood to sing, the person behind them would put a hymnal in the seat of the person in front of them. When the person in front sat down, they sat on the book and would have to pull it out from under them. This was not a big deal, just a little prank. Another prank was to switch seats. Before the service started, students would find a seat and put their Bible and personal belongings there, and go to the restroom or talk to others away from their seat. Some students would get the personal belongings and move them to another row or section, just to play and pick with the other student. Although this was a common event in one church, it was quite different when done at a new church. A MC was seen moving a friend's belongings to another section of seats. One mom and dad saw this happen to their daughter and accused the MC of being hateful and shunning their daughter. This was never the intention. But the girl's parents simply didn't think it was funny or harmless. There had to be a big meeting to smooth it out.

Another crazy situation happened when an MC was seen holding a teenage girl's newborn child. The teen belonged to a single mom and had a child when she was 17. The MC was in Sunday school class with the pregnant teen and watched her go through the struggles of a teen pregnancy. They weren't really friends. A few months after the child was born, the teen mom brought her child to church. Naturally, adults and teens alike wanted to see the baby. The MC had her turn holding the baby and saying how beautiful it was. Later, a church member accused the MC of condoning and supporting teen pregnancy, and the only reason was because she held the baby and was nice to the teen mom. Being a teen mom is hard enough without having to deal with haters. This MC found herself in a no-win situation.

One pastor changed careers from pastoral ministry to a secular job. When asked how it was going he said, "Very Well." He said people only got mad at him about twice a year, but that while in ministry, someone was always mad about something. This is both disheartening and a strange way for the body of Christ to act. MCs hear much about their dad, that is, if they attend a business meeting. One former minister said, and his wife agreed, that "business meetings were the reason MCs walk away from the church. MCs get disillusioned by the SINinster words and actions of church members towards their dads during hate-filled, self-absorbing business meetings." Many churches have wonderful meetings where they discuss plans for ministering to more hurting people.

QUESTIONS TO CONSIDER

1.   What questions have you answered over and over again to church members?

2.   Have church members asked you what side of an argument you were on?

3. What expectations are placed on MCs that are not placed on the children of "regular" church members?

4. Has your dad ever used your life experiences as a sermon illustration?

5. What have you been unfairly accused of?

CHAPTER NINE
BEING THE CHILD OF A MISSIONARY

Following are two brief excerpts from a missionary's child and from missionaries that are telling the story of what it was like for their children to be on the mission field with them. Sometimes, the situations were not only hard to deal with, but dangerous and life- threatening for the entire family.

Undisclosed Country - The following is from a family serving in an undisclosed country for 20 years.

Our family answered God's call to go to an unreached people when our children were 11, 8 and 4 years of age. We prayed as a family and decided to give up our country's——————— way of life–pets, sports, friends and family—to go share the love of God with those who had not yet heard the gospel. Our children loved going on adventures, so we set off for a grand adventure!

Although we tried, nothing could prepare us for what was to come. We packed all our home, school and personal belongings into 11 footlockers.

Each of the children had one footlocker in which to pack their most prized possessions–Legos, models, games and books. One footlocker contained decorations for each American holiday so we could honor and remind the children of the celebrations of our homeland. When our plane landed in our country of service, soldiers carrying machine guns lined the runway. We walked through throngs of strangely dressed people who were all gawking at us and speaking to us in a language we did not know. Co-workers were waiting for us just outside the airport to take us to our new home in a rural desert region. The truck bounced down rutted dirt roads lined with open sewer ditches, passing donkeys, goats, bicycles and more staring people to our cinder block house with a wall around it. That night we ate food we had never had before and tried to sleep to new sounds wafting through open windows of donkeys braying, babies crying and nearby families talking and washing dishes outside. Sunrise awakened us to the sound of a sheep herd busily eating at the garbage dump across from our house. As we ate a breakfast of local-made bread and buffalo milk (one must acquire the taste for such!) we asked the children what they thought of their new home. The older kids tried to be kind in their responses, but the youngest proclaimed with his fingers pinching his nose, "It stinks here, and I want to go home!" We were the first Americans to ever live among the people of this particular village. In order to be culturally appropriate, our family wore the clothes and coverings used by the local villagers. We also followed the cultural rules, which meant giving up some of our "rights" we were accustomed to in America. For example, when visitors came for tea, the whole family was required to sit in the room while they were there, usually for a one-hour visit. Children were to sit quietly and still while the adults talked. Our children considered it an impossible task but tried their best!

The adults, while wary, were kind and welcoming. The street kids, however, carried out the prejudice they had been taught concerning foreigners. This was especially difficult on our children as they tried to go out and make friends. In our first weeks of language learning, one of the first phrases we learned was, "We are new here and we want to be your friend." One day after morning devotions from Matthew 5, our two sons walked down the street to buy some bread. A group of boys surrounded them and threw rocks at them as our sons tried to escape. The boys came into the house crying and angry. We were all reminded of the morning Scripture reading immediately: "Blessed are you when people insult you and persecute you …love your enemies and pray for those who persecute you (Mt 5:11 & 44)." We prayed and asked God to forgive them and thought of a way to bless them. Our sons were not thrilled about the idea, but we went back to the place where they had been attacked. An old man was at the corner, so we spoke our newly learned phrase, "We are new here and want to be your friend." Then we used hand motions to tell him about the rock-throwing incident. He called the group of attackers to him and told them to be kind to our sons. Then our sons spoke the phrase to them and invited their new "friends" to come to our house for cookies and tea. We made up a new game for them to play. Since we knew they were good at throwing rocks, we drew a bulls-eye circle on our cinder block wall and let them take turns throwing at the bulls-eye at varying distances. They were very good at it! We gave an extra cookie to the winner. A year later, that winner came and asked us to pray for his mother because she was very sick. He really had become a friend who trusted the love of God. Our sons learned how to take

God at His word and apply it to daily challenges.

Our sons were soon playing soccer, cricket and flying pigeons, and learning the new language as they played with their friends. The pigeons really helped us get to know all the neighbors when they landed on every roof in the village except ours! When our children were able to compete and win at games, they discovered that the new culture was based on anger and revenge.

Demonstrating good sportsmanship and forgiveness was an important part of what we came to call "Play Evangelism." When one of his friends became angry with our son and wrote him a hate letter, our son wrote a letter of kindness and friendship in return. Within one week, both the friend and his father came to our house to ask more about the love of God. It was inspiring to see our children develop a passion for sharing their faith with their friends.

Our kids joined us on prayer walks in our neighborhood as well. We would pray for each and every neighbor to know God's love. We prayed for healing from a disease that was in the village. We prayed for peace in the country. One day a local friend came to the house to say her husband had been taken hostage and a ransom was demanded for his release. She came to ask us to pay the ransom. I told her we could not pay it but that we would pray for his safe release. Three days later, she came to the house again to tell us that she had a dream the night before of a man in glowing white holding her husband's hand walking him down the road back to our village! I immediately exclaimed that was Jesus and that her husband would be home soon! When she left, I fell to my knees and said, "Lord, I just put Your great name on the line! Please deliver her husband! Two weeks later, her husband returned to the village safe and unharmed! Our family became known as the praying family whose prayers are answered! Our children had the opportunity to see the mighty power of God as He answered the prayers of His people!

The nearest medical help to our village was a plane flight away which took two days. Early on, our family struggled with an ongoing illness called giardia. At one point, our oldest child became sick with amoebic dysentery. After taking local medicine, he went into shock and began having trouble breathing. We held his hands and asked God to heal him and spare his life. The Lord was gracious to restore his health, and our children learned first-hand to trust God for their healing rather than solely trusting in medical insurance and doctors.

Our children learned to trust God to be their protector and shield as well. There were frequent bombings and attacks on foreigners in our country of service. At one point, because of political issues, a bounty was placed on the heads of all Americans. Our family was grateful when our local friends would laugh and tell us they would not take the bounty! It was a blessing to be able to rest on God's hand of protection. There were times when we had to evacuate, but we were always able to return to our village. Our children understood the dangers of our location. Some of our co-workers were kidnapped; some of our national co-workers were put in prison for their faith. Some of the expats with whom we worked were martyred as they served the peoples who killed them. We learned to be sober minded and vigilant, understanding that we have an enemy who seeks to destroy us, as I Peter 5:8 warns. But our kids learned to trust the God who has written every day ordained for them in His book (Ps 139) and to reckon on His watch guard over them.

There were no fast food restaurants in the village; no movie theaters or malls. So, our children learned to make their own fun! One favorite was the re-enactment of the Olympics in our yard. There were at least six competitive events and ribbons were awarded to the winners! Each of the kids had good hobbies to keep them busy as well. We got a dog in our second year, and that really made us feel like we were home. Then came the cats, birds, turtles and fish! And we played lots of family board games when it was too hot to be outside. Much of the time, we were without electricity. Summer temperatures inside the house went to one hundred degrees. In the winter, our water bottles would freeze beside our beds. The food supply in the bazaar was seasonal and the children learned to be thankful for the food that was available. Our work was 24/7—whenever the locals knocked on our door, we tried to be available to them. Oftentimes our children had to wait with their own needs until we were free to help them. So, the kids developed a close bond as siblings who cared for each other; although there were the usual complaints that siblings will have! They became really good at enjoying the moment and making the most of every opportunity. Whether it was creating water propulsion rockets or making music or training birds, there was always something fun on the horizon!

There were wonderful times of family togetherness. There were also times that were not so wonderful when our children had to see their parents when we were not at our best—times when we argued or times of lack of faith or times of downright fleshly willfulness; our children saw it all. Because our home was small, they could also hear all of our discussions. Our children had to realize early on that their parents were frail human beings who often fail and must go to God for forgiveness. They saw that when we don't rely on God, we fall flat. There were also times of deep discouragement when we did not feel we could remain in such a dark place. At one point, we had a family meeting to discuss leaving or staying. Our son said he thought we had made a mistake to go to such a hard place. We reminded him that we had prayed as a family and decided God was leading us there. His reply was, "Then God made a mistake!" As a family, we decided to ask God to help us stay one week. Each week after that, we would ask the Lord to help us through one more week. And He did! He gave us grace for each new day. Then one day we realized we had forgotten to have a family meeting! We proved true the verse in I Corinthians 1 that God uses the weak things of this world for His glory! We can say with Paul that we glory in our weakness because then God is made strong.

The children also made friends with the kids of ex-patriots from other countries that lived in the city near our village. It served to broaden their worldview as they got to learn about different nationalities. Once a week, we would gather in a home for worship with other believers in the city. There was no youth group. There were no amenities. The worship time included singing with guitar accompaniment, prayer and reading from

God's word. Our children had the privilege to hear stories from all over the world of God's faithfulness and blessing in the lives of those who follow Him. Their faith was strengthened by the testimony of the other families. It was further strengthened as we watched the Lord grow His church where there had not been one before! Worship becomes so real and so personal when we are in dark places, and it is easy to recognize our deep need of the Lord to intervene on our behalf.

All of our children were home schooled in their early years. The greatest challenge was bringing in enough books to keep them satisfied in their reading. It is such a blessing today that families can supply their children with an ample supply of reading materials for each child on electronic reading devices! As our children got older, each of them chose a different path for their education. Based on their personalities and individual needs, we prayed with each of our kids to find the path God had for them. Our oldest son decided to go to boarding school. There were two school options for him—one in the mountains and one on an island. As we prayed about which one to choose, the Lord showed us in Scripture that our son should go "to the sea" because the mountains "would have a 'rain of fire'." We obeyed that direction from the Lord to send our son to the island. Two years later, gunmen attacked the school in the mountains. God miraculously protected the students there—none were injured. But we were so grateful for His direction earlier for our son! Our second child stayed with us and home schooled until his final year. He then stayed with friends in the States to graduate. Our youngest child was able to attend a school in the city to which we relocated. In our experience, each child is different, and his needs are unique. The Lord was faithful to provide for each in a unique way. Whether they are independent and desire to go away to school or prefer to remain close to family for their schooling, parents can help their children determine the path God has for them.

Our children also traveled to other countries and learned to navigate in different cultures. It became a habit to look on the map in the booklet on the airplane to discover what ocean or how many countries we would fly over in route to our destination. They also tried to learn some of the phrases in the language of the country during the vacation. We also allowed our kids to take the lead going through passport and ticket counters and locating airport terminals on our trips so they would be self-sufficient when traveling alone at some point. Each of them did take international trips alone in their teenage years.

The most difficult trip to prepare for was our first trip back to America after four years of being away. Our oldest child remembered his home and friends, but our youngest child did not remember anything about America. He had more identity with our country of service than he did with the country we call home. As their parents, it was hard for us to understand because we had both grown up in the same hometown all our lives. Our identity is firmly rooted in American culture. We were all in for a few surprises!

Upon arriving in America, the friend who picked us up whipped into a McDonald's drive-through to get us all a cold drink. As she placed the order, our youngest son leaned toward me and whispered, "Why is she talking to a box? We can't get drinks from there!" When we got to the grandparents' home, they wrinkled their noses as they hugged us and asked if we would like to get a shower while they washed our clothes! It seems the smell of our "stinky" country had come with us! As our older son tried to tell his friends about his overseas experiences, they quickly changed the subject to American topics of which he was unaware. Our middle child was quiet and uneasy as he tried to take in the grocery store with all its choices of foods. We left in tears having bought nothing as we remembered the thousands of starving refugees in our service country. I stood staring at the gas pump trying to figure out how to use an automated payment machine. America was going to take some getting used to! Kids were using pop culture phrases that our children had not heard and did not know the meaning of. Our youngest child did not know how to ride an elevator or escalator. School proved to be a challenge because he had never sat in a public classroom and had no concept of classroom rules. Big churches were very loud and scary after our simple house church. We found ourselves feeling like outsiders in our home country. This is a common occurrence among missionary kids. They are not only American, but they are not fully from the service country either. They are actually a third culture of children who have lived in more than one country, known as "third culture kids" or TCK's.

Eastern European Child of a Missionary

This story is from a missionary's child in an eastern European country:

Technically, I've been a missionary pastor's child for about 10 years now, although I am 20. This is because we started our church 10 years ago, and that was when my dad started his ministry as a pastor. I think I am very fortunate because I haven't really had many negative experiences about being a missionary pastor's child. I know in many churches this is not the case and these children live under constant pressure.

The thing I'd like to highlight as a major aspect of my dad being a missionary is I can see the life of the missionary a lot more than anyone else in the church—except for my mom. I can see that he is not that holy-and-never-exhausted, always-on-fire man we might expect.

He is as human as I am. Sometimes he goes to bed at two and gets up at six to finish his sermon. Sometimes he is frustrated by how people can't understand what it means to shift our focus from ourselves to others. Sometimes he spends hours to correct our mistakes and teach us the principles of the Kingdom of God. Sometimes he's hopeless and feels like his own son has let him down for the thousandth time, although he believed him again. And in the meantime he is leading a church, he is teaching people, he is giving his heart and energy to the people who keep hurting him. He never loses sight of the hope and dream God has given him. Week by week, day by day he does his best for the church and for those who don't yet know God.

I most sincerely admire him. It probably has to do with the fact that I am his son, but also with the things I can see in his life. I think it is amazing and remarkable how he is carrying the fire of God in his heart in spite of all the circumstances that encourage him to let go of it. His faith, strength and determination rooted in God's truth is going to be an inspiration for me as long as I live.

So, being a missionary's child allows me to see how my dad, the pastor of my church, is a human being like anyone else with feelings, dreams, troubles, ups and downs. Also, it allows me to see what a man of faith he is and amazes me how he cannot be crushed by the enemy no matter what. This is such a blessing to me and I will always be so grateful for this.

The following poem written by a missionary's child aptly describes the inner struggle of most TCK's:

Colors
by Whitni Thomas, MK (1991)

I grew up in a Yellow country
but my parents are Blue.
I'm Blue.
Or at least, that is what they told me.
But I play with the Yellows.
I went to school with the Yellows.
I spoke the Yellow language.
I even dressed and appeared to be Yellow.
Then I moved to the Blue land.

Now I go to school with the Blues.

I speak the Blue language.

I even dress and look Blue.

But deep down, inside me, something's Yellow.

I love the Blue country.

But my ways are tinted with Yellow.

When I am in the Blue land,

I want to be Yellow.

When I am in the Yellow land,

I want to be Blue.

Why can't I be both?

A place where I can be me.

A place where I can be green.

I just want to be green.

The emotional turmoil going on inside returning missionary kids is common. It is good for parents, families and churches to be aware of the internal struggle with which they are dealing and to know some ways to help. The best start is to let the kids know before they return that there will be a struggle–that it is common to most TCK's–so that they are not caught off guard by it. Most sending agencies have a re-entry program for returning missionary families in order to give each member some time to acclimate to life in America once again. Families of TCK's can be aware and be prepared to listen to stories and lifestyles that sound very foreign. It really helps the TCK if there is a "home base" to which they return each time they come back to America. In this way, they build an idea of a hometown even though they don't live there all the time. It provides stability for world-traveling kids. Churches who welcome missionary families into their fellowship can provide informed peer buddies who introduce the TCK to the rest of the youth group and help them to fit into the flow of activities. Many MKs return with struggles of faith and could benefit from the counsel of a youth pastor.

Instant electronic communication technology has connected the world in amazing ways and poses both a blessing and a danger to missionary families. It is wonderful to be able to face-time and instant message with our families in the States even when we are on the other side of the world. It is a wonderful tool for staying in touch with our families and churches as well. It can help bridge the information gap that TCK's deal with. They can keep up with all the latest songs and news from home so they no longer feel so isolated. Yet, the focus of missions is letting go of one culture to fully embrace and become an accepted outsider of another culture. There is some necessary heartache of separation from old ties before we begin to make deep friendships with people of another culture. And deep friendships are the source of the gospel being shared effectively. The danger of constant contact with the home country is that the missionary family does not fully engage the new culture and so does not develop good methods to communicate the gospel. Therefore, while missionary families and missionary kids recognize and utilize the benefits of the new technology, they can also be intentional about creating paths down which the gospel can travel in their country of service.

After attending college, each of our children has chosen careers to serve our country and encourage others through praise music. They still find excitement in unusual places and still enjoy being together. We are most grateful that they have chosen to follow the Lord.

APPENDIX A
MOTHERS: THE HIDDEN STRENGTH

They are our mothers. To us, they are on a par with our fathers. People always make MCs feel as though they are the product of just one parent. Moms of MCs and wives of ministers are incredibly strong. They are always the person in the background, playing second fiddle. It is the mom from which MCs draw strength, advice and nurture. MCs also get advice and response to professional needs from dad...especially, if the mom wasn't a career or professional woman. People who have met both parents usually ask first about the mom. Most pastors' wives are very smart and so witty and so overshadowed. MC moms live for their children and their husband and that other bride, the bride of Christ, the church. Although they may never go out and do anything professionally, the way they run a house is sheer art, and that is not so easy. It gets dumped on her a lot, and it's just not easy.

A common experience of pastors' wives is being overlooked. I saw an example of this at a conference. At the conference, a man greeted the minister "dad" as the family entered the building, and almost before the family had gotten in the door, he brought over another friend of his to be introduced to the minister, totally unaware, it seemed, of the mother's presence. The man neither acknowledged nor introduced her. Of course, the minister was quick to introduce his wife and include her.

When a minister goes to a graduation or holiday party, he's the celebrity, so he's always the center of attention. It never seems fair for the minister's wife to be in the background in those situations. Even when she stands beside her husband, the minister still has to make sure others don't ignore her.

Pastor's wives get frustrated. When her husband is starting out and his church is growing and progressing nicely, a pastor's wife is excited for him. But ultimately, it is important for each person to have their own sense of self-esteem. One cannot operate entirely out of their husband's successes. It is important to have internal self-respect, self-esteem and identity. It is important what people think about the minister's wife. Yet, no matter what others think, her husband and children love her unconditionally and understand who she is.

In the home when the dad missed dinner—again—the mom must take the high ground and explain to the children why dad is gone. A MCs mom must never let the children hear her say in frustration, "Your dad is not here again; I get so tired of him missing dinner. I work so hard to have a good dinner prepared and everything just right, and he isn't here." MCs pick up on and mimic the attitude and spirit of the mom in situations like this. When the MC becomes a teenager and a little more independent they may resent the church. That is not what ministers and their wives want.

QUESTIONS TO CONSIDER

1. Have you ever seen your pastor's wife play second fiddle?

2. Would you rather your pastor's wife to be in the background or to be his partner?

3. Does the pastor's wife have a right to her own goals and aspirations?

4. What do you think about the pastor's wife who is not involved in the church but who has her own career?

NOTES

NOTES

NOTES

NOTES

NOTES

NOTES

NOTES

NOTES

NOTES

NOTES

NOTES

NOTES

NOTES

NOTES

WHAT OTHERS ARE SAYING
ABOUT THIS BOOK

There are precious few books that address the issues of being raised in the "fishbowl" of living as the child of a minister. None that I have ever read dealt with this issue as clearly and adequately as Steve's book. Coupled with his 25 years, so far, in raising children in minis▮▮and the many ministers' families he has worked with, allows him to have a unique advantage in looking at the problems and solutions of life in the fishbowl of ministry. A 2006 study by Focus on the Family revealed that nearly 80 percent of the children of ministers will develop depression resulting in a need for professional biblical counseling. Steve has laid out the problems and steps to take in resolving the issues, following clear biblical truths that face this issue head on. This is a must read for any minister who has or is planning to raise a family.

Johnny L. Derouen, PhD
Professor of Student Ministry | School of Church and Family Ministries
Southwestern Baptist Theological Seminary

Steve Maltempi understands MCs (ministers' children). He understands them as a dad. He understands them as a youth pastor. He understands them through his research. And he understands them because he creates large events to bring together lots of them. Vocational ministers who read the book will tend to say, "I can use those insights with my kids tonight." MCs who read the book will tend to say, "Finally, someone understands me." Caring church members who read the book will tend to say, "Those are new insights that will cause me to do some things differently." In every case, Christ will receive glory.

Richard Ross, PhD
Professor of Student Ministry | School of Church and Family Ministries
Southwestern Baptist Theological Seminary
www.RichardARoss.com

Steve and Joy Maltempi have pulled back the curtain into a rare look at the home of a minister. I have known Steve since his time at seminary, and I am not surprised by the candid, raw, and excellent words he put on the pages of In the Fish Bowl. Unlike some books in this genre, he does not beat up a pastor for not spending enough time with family, for not taking time off, etc. He does warn us against "spiritual water-boarding"—a term that perfectly describes a trap we have all fallen into. From the candid personal comments from a small-town setting to the courageous discussion from career missionaries in a dangerous place, this book is just right. Ministers need to read it. Ministers' kids need to read it. Church leadership needs to read it. And this seminary professor needed to read it.

R. Allen Jackson, PhD
Professor of Youth Education and Collegiate Ministry
Director of the Youth Ministry Institute
New Orleans Baptist Theological Seminary